why the dreyfus affair matters

yale

university

press

new haven

and

london

louis

begley

why the

dreyfus affair

matters

Published with assistance from the foundation established in memory of Philip Hamilton McMillan of the Class of 1894, Yale College.

Designed by Nancy Ovedovitz and set in Adobe Garamond type by Integrated Publishing Solutions. Printed in the United States of America.

The Library of Congress has cataloged the hardcover edition as follows:
Begley, Louis.
Why the Dreyfus Affair matters / Louis Begley. — 1st ed.
    p. cm. — (Why X matters)
Includes bibliographical references and index.
ISBN 978-0-300-12532-0 (cloth: alk. paper)
1. Dreyfus, Alfred, 1859–1935. 2. Dreyfus, Alfred, 1859–1935—Influence. 3. Trials (Treason)—Political aspects—France.
4. Antisemitism—France—History—19th century.
5. France—History—Third Republic, 1870–1940. I. Title.
DC354.B44 2009
944.051′2—dc22   2009005140
ISBN 978-0-300-16814-3 (pbk.)

A catalogue record for this book is available from the British Library.

10 9 8 7 6 5 4 3 2 1

also by louis begley

For Robert, and later also for Jacob and Elisabeth

contents

preface

I was making the final changes in the manuscript of this book today, the day after the inauguration of President Barack Obama, when I learned from an article in the *Miami Herald* that the Pentagon prosecutor at Guantánamo Naval Base had filed a motion the previous afternoon, eight hours after the president had taken the oath of office, to stay for 120 days the war crimes trial of the alleged September 11th mastermind, Khalid Sheikh Mohammed. The purpose of the motion was to give the new administration time to study ongoing war on terror prosecutions. According to a military commission spokesman at Guantánamo, similar delays will be sought in all pending cases. Mohammed is one of five detainees, all allegedly involved in planning the attacks on the World Trade Center and the Pentagon, in whose cases the government is seeking the death penalty. The charges against the sixth detainee in this group, Mohammed al-Qahtani, said to be the missing twentieth hijacker who was denied entry into the

United States and thus did not take part in the attacks, have been dismissed. According to a recent interview with Judge Susan J. Crawford, the top Bush administration official in charge of deciding whether to bring Guantánamo detainees to trial, al-Qahtani had been tortured by the U.S. military, and she would therefore never permit him to be put on trial.

In his Inaugural Address, with former president George W. Bush and former vice president Richard B. Cheney sitting a few rows behind him, President Obama said: "As for our common defense, we reject as false the choice between our safety and our ideals. Our Founding Fathers, faced with perils that we can scarcely imagine, drafted a charter to assure the rule of law and the rights of man—a charter expanded by the blood of generations. Those ideals still light the world, and we will not give them up for expedience' sake." Thus in two lofty sentences the president rejected the Bush-Cheney heritage of trampling on America's international obligations under both the Geneva Conventions and the U.N. Convention Against Torture while at the same time evading or violating the laws and Constitution of the United States. An end had come to the era of dragnet detentions and mistreatment or worse of alleged enemy combatants, and secret CIA prisons. President Obama had taken the first step toward redeeming his campaign pledge to close Guantánamo and bring the United States back under the rule of law.

One supposes that the news of Senator Obama's victory on November 4, 2008, must have spread from cell to cell in Guantánamo—except perhaps to those in which detainees, some of them shackled, are held in solitary confinement—and one can imagine the stirring of hope among the prisoners. One can even more easily imagine the joy with which the news of the stay of the trials before the military commissions has been greeted. Certainly, those detainees who know that there is reason to bring them to trial cannot expect to evade that outcome. But the trials will be before U.S. federal courts or properly constituted military tribunals. In either case, the defendants will be under the protection of U.S. laws and the U.S. Constitution, and they will be afforded substantially the same protections as defendants charged with crimes who are tried before U.S. courts.

One can allow one's imagination roam further, to Devil's Island, where on the afternoon of June 5, 1899, after almost five years of brutally punitive solitary confinement, Alfred Dreyfus learned that his 1894 conviction for treason by a court-martial in Paris had been overturned by the Cour de Cassation, the highest court of France. The communication he received from the prison administration did not say that the Court was setting him free; rather, he was being remanded for a new court-martial— but that was all he had asked for. This former French artillery captain, stripped of his military grade and condemned to perpetual imprisonment on a tropical and insalubrious island, wanted above all to be cleared by a jury of French officers of the hideous crime of treason for which he had been convicted, and thus to save his own and his children's honor. He knew that he was innocent. Indeed, no sane person would have thought otherwise. He had no motive for the crime, and the guilty verdict had come after a trial from which the public and the press had been excluded. So far as he knew, it had been based on nothing more than a single piece of paper to which nothing except an alleged similarity of handwritings linked him, a similarity on which handwriting experts could not agree. The fellow staff officer who had testified against him had perjured himself. The military jury before which he was tried had been intimidated by the army chiefs who had accused him. Even so, the jury—but this was a fact of which he was still unaware—had convicted him only after the minister or war had caused to be given them in secret altered documents, of whose existence neither Dreyfus nor his counsel were informed.

Times and circumstances change. Some Guantánamo detainees may be as innocent as Dreyfus; some surely are not. But before January 20, Guantánamo detainees could look forward only to trials that would be as unfair and lacking in protections for the defendant as the court-martial that convicted Dreyfus. The Dreyfus case became the Dreyfus Affair, which tore France apart for long years after the case had come to an end and Captain Dreyfus had been fully exonerated. Steps taken by President Obama may spare the United States similar bitter strife, burnish its soiled image, and offer a path to freedom to those Guantánamo detainees who deserve it.

New York, January 21, 2009

acknowledgments

I wish to express my profound gratitude to the following:

Professor Robert O. Paxton, who selflessly read my manuscript while on a rustic vacation.

My old friends Joel Conarroe, James H. Duffy, and Donald Hall, who as with so many of my other books provided invaluable comments.

My editor Ileene Smith at Yale University Press, for her astute judgment and invariably good humor.

Susan Laity at Yale University Press, for the meticulous care of my manuscript.

My friend Lisa A. Kofod, who guided me through the labyrinth of word processing.

My friend and German translator, Dr. Christa Krüger, who has caught more mistakes in my manuscripts, including this one, than I can count.

Antoine Kirry, a Paris partner in the law firm from which I retired after forty-five years of service, who confirmed my guesses about French law and procedure.

My son Adam, who extricated me from a literary trap I had set for myself.

My stepson Robert Dujarric, for his indefatigable attention to my manuscript, and for setting me straight about more than one problem in French history. This work is dedicated to him and to my French grandchildren, Jacob and Elisabeth.

why the dreyfus affair matters

Police photograph of Alfred Dreyfus taken immediately after the military degradation ceremony, 1895 (Harry Ransom Humanities Research Center, The University of Texas at Austin. Photograph by Alphonse Bertillon.)

"If they haven't been ordered to convict him, he will be acquitted this evening"

At nine o'clock on Monday morning, October 15, 1894, a French artillery officer serving as a trainee with the army's General Staff reported to the Ministry of War building on rue Saint-Dominique, in the aristocratic faubourg Saint-Germain of Paris, obeying an order delivered to his apartment the preceding Saturday. It had summoned officer trainees to an inspection by the General Staff. The morning hour was unusual; inspections routinely took place in the evening. So was the requirement that the officer be in mufti. To his surprise, on arrival he was met by Major Georges Picquart, who said he would escort him to the office of the chief, General Charles Le Mouton de Boisdeffre. The officer's surprise was compounded when he realized that neither the general nor any other officer trainee was present. Instead, he saw an officer who introduced himself as Major Armand Mercier du Paty de Clam and three unknown civilians. Du Paty explained that the general would be back shortly and, pleading injury to his right hand, asked the officer to take down a letter, which he dictated from a document that would soon become infamous as the *bordereau* (account). The letter finished, du Paty drew himself up to his considerable full height, put his hand on the officer's shoulder, and bellowed: "In the name of the law, I put you under arrest; you are accused of high treason." The civilians pounced on the officer and searched him.

The artillery officer was, of course, Captain Alfred Dreyfus, who became in the decade that followed one of the best-known men in Europe, if not in the world. The three civilians were the chief of Sûreté générale, the police attached to the Ministry of the Interior, which was often entrusted with political tasks; his secretary; and Félix Gribelin, the archivist at the Section de statistique (Statistics Section), the intelligence and counterintelligence unit of the General Staff. Concealed behind a curtain and watching the proceedings was Major Joseph Henry, also of the Statistics Section. Henry took over after the arrest and escorted Dreyfus to the military prison on rue du Cherche-midi, a very long street on the Left Bank that stretches from the sixth to the fifteenth arrondissement.

So it happened that with only one exception the principal actors of the drama about to commence were all onstage for its first act. Missing was Major Ferdinand Walsin-Esterhazy. Also off-stage, but waiting in the wings, were the top brass: General Auguste Mercier, the minister of war; Boisdeffre; Arthur Gonse, deputy chief of staff; and Lieutenant Colonel Jean Sandherr, chief of the Statistics Section, who reported to Gonse. Over the course of the next five years, the three generals would inspire, encourage, dictate, and sanction by their authority the illegal and often bizarre actions of their subordinates.

The events leading up to the arrest have been related many times. On July 24, 1894, Major Esterhazy, a French officer, offered to sell important French military secrets to the German military attaché in Paris, Lieutenant Colonel Maximilian von Schwartzkoppen. Esterhazy was a descendant of the illegitimate French branch of the ancient and illustrious Austro-Hungarian family, which had never acknowledged the French offshoot. An amoral sociopath, Esterhazy lied, intrigued, and swindled obsessively. He was chronically in debt; his wife, a French aristocrat whose family winced when they let her marry him, had found it necessary to take legal measures to protect her small personal fortune from his depredations. Schwartzkoppen had hesitated about the wisdom of employing a French officer as a spy, but, concerned about important opportunities he might otherwise miss, he had consulted his superiors in Berlin. With their approval, he accepted Esterhazy's offer. According to Schwartzkoppen, in the course of an hour and a half's subsequent conversation at the embassy on September 1, Esterhazy told him much that was of interest and gave him an artillery manual and memoranda he had written on the subject of the new short 120-

millimeter cannon being developed by the French, French troop positions and modifications in the battle order of artillery units, and plans for the imminent invasion and colonization of Madagascar.[1] The delivery of these documents was memorialized in the bordereau, which was unsigned and undated and written on onionskin paper. The reference to the 120-millimeter cannon was particularly important because a huge effort was being made by the French military to develop a weapon that would erase the advantage in artillery ordnance that had contributed to Prussia's victory in the Franco-Prussian War of 1870. Shortly after its receipt by the attaché, the bordereau reached the Statistics Section through "la voie normale" (usual channel).[2] This euphemism referred to Madame Marie Bastian, a cleaning woman at the German Embassy who was in the pay of the Section. One of her daily duties was to empty Schwartzkoppen's wastebasket and throw the contents into the furnace. Instead, she delivered any papers she found in it to a representative of the Statistics Section. Most frequently this was Major Henry, one of whose tasks was to deal regularly with the large and motley clan of corrupt servants, concierges, and double agents employed by the Section.

That had been as well the trajectory of the bordereau, which came into Henry's hands on September 26 along with a batch of other documents. It had been torn into pieces, but because it was in French—unlike most documents from Schwartzkoppen's wastebasket—Henry was able put it back together without the help of his German-speaking colleague Captain Jules Lauth. The bordereau's importance was apparent to him as soon as he had read it. The next day he showed the reconstituted document to his chief, Sandherr. The range of secrets being sold led Sandherr and his General Staff colleagues to assume that the traitor must be a knowledgeable insider working at the ministry. There had been other recent leaks of secrets that had seemed to emanate from there, and the Statistics Section had been investigating them without success. The bordereau underscored the vital importance of finding the traitor.

The new investigation was conducted with almost clownish incompetence. The handwriting on the bordereau was compared with the handwriting on other intercepted documents in the Section's files. It did not match any of them. What's more, none of the heads of the four General Staff departments recognized the handwriting as belonging to one of their junior officers. As a result, after a little over a week, the effort to identify the author of the bordereau was about to be abandoned. The situation changed dramatically on October 6 when, like a demon ex machina, Lieutenant Colonel Albert d'Aboville returned from vacation. Newly promoted, he was pleased with the opportunity to show off, and promptly announced that he had found the solution that had eluded his colleagues. It consisted in zeroing in on the profile of the culprit. According to d'Aboville, in order to be able to provide data relating to the cannon, the author had to be an artillery officer. Moreover, because of the variety of the other subjects enumerated in the bordereau, he had to be someone familiar with the entire spectrum of the General Staff's work. In d'Aboville's opinion, this narrowed the field to officer trainees because they rotated from department to department and became familiar with the work of each. Although cockily self-assured, d'Aboville was wrong: Esterhazy was an infantry officer serving with a line regiment whose knowledge of the subjects enumerated in the bordereau was limited and superficial. This had not deterred him from addressing them; he wrote well and with brio and was accustomed to making his readers think he knew more than he did.

A list of trainees was produced, and the name Dreyfus immediately stood out. As an artillery officer trainee, he fit d'Aboville's specifications. Moreover, both d'Aboville and his immediate superior, Colonel Pierre-Elie Fabre, knew Dreyfus and disliked him. Fabre, in fact, had recently given Dreyfus a negative review, in which he had recognized Dreyfus's intelligence and talent but condemned his pretentiousness, unsatisfactory attitude, and faults of character. A sample of Dreyfus's handwriting was called for: it seemed to those present to resemble the handwriting on the bordereau. The resemblance should not have been surprising; at that time the slanted, highly cursive script was taught at every school. Gonse and Boisdeffre were alerted, and Boisdeffre briefed the minister of war, General Mercier. Du Paty's interest in graphology was known to his colleagues on the General Staff, and he was asked for his views. After studying the handwritings over the weekend, du Paty confirmed the conclusion reached by the group: the handwritings were identical. Dreyfus was the traitor.

Dreyfus, the only Jewish officer trainee on the General Staff, was fated to be singled out. Anti-Semitism—of the traditional religious sort, as well as economic and racial—had reached an intensity never before experienced in France. Although they had maintained correct professional relations with Dreyfus, the officers preparing to accuse Dreyfus were anti-Semites. If only for that reason, they disliked him. At the same time it must be recognized that Sandherr, his colleagues, and their superiors were not inventing a crime or looking for a Jew to be the scapegoat. The bordereau was a real document, a real traitor was at work, and it was a routine counterintelligence task of the Statistics Section to find him. That is what these officers were attempting. The superficial resemblance between Esterhazy's and Dreyfus's handwritings was likewise real. But Dreyfus's being a Jew made it easier for his fellow officers to accuse him. He was not "one of them"; according to anti-Semitic propaganda, as a Jew he wasn't really French. Therefore the stain on the honor of the General Staff of treason having been committed by a French officer assigned to it would be avoided. Dreyfus's presence on the General Staff, even if only provisional, was an anomaly—and would have been such on the general staff of any European army. In the opinion of traditionalist officers, the unfortunate aberration went to prove that the modern recruiting reforms in the General Staff, modeled on the German practice of relying on competitive examinations, had been ill advised. Under the cooptation system previously in use, a Jewish officer would never have been admitted into the precincts of the General Staff or have had the opportunity to spy on its work.

A little over a week after Dreyfus's arrest, which was still being kept secret, Sandherr visited Maurice Paléologue at the Ministry of Foreign Affairs to bring him confidentially up to date on the most sensitive matter then being dealt with by the Statistics Section, one which had already given rise to a good deal of gossip.

Paléologue was a young diplomat—he was twenty-seven at the time—with the rank of embassy secretary. He was attached to the ministry's own Intelligence Section and was the de facto representative of the Ministry of Foreign Affairs to the Statistics Section and, more generally, to the General Staff. Descended from the Paléologue emperors of Byzantium, he occupied a brilliant position in Parisian society that made it possible for him to be on terms of easy friendship with his minister, the president of the republic, and many other much older men in positions of power. Paléologue kept a journal in which he recorded Sandherr's remarks: "The officer charged with treason is a Jew, Captain Alfred Dreyfus, who has just finished a long training period in the various departments of the General Staff. That is why he could obtain so much information. In addition, his indiscreet curiosity, his constant snooping, his air of mystery, and finally his false and conceited character, 'in which one recognizes all the pride and all the ignominy of his race,' have made him suspect for a long time."[3]

The statement that Dreyfus had been under suspicion before the discovery of the bordereau and the comparison of handwritings was an outright fabrication and illustrates the effort Sandherr and his cohort had made—and would continue to make—to validate retrospectively the charge of treason and fit Dreyfus into an anti-Semitic stereotype. The prejudice against Dreyfus, on the other hand, was real and explains why the case against him was mishandled. If Dreyfus had been a typical General Staff officer—a Catholic and an offshoot of a military or aristocratic family or a member of the solid Catholic or Protestant bourgeoisie—considerably more objective and expert scrutiny of the two handwritings, as well as a motive for the crime, would have been required before he was charged. But Dreyfus's accusers could say to themselves that he was a man without a country and, like all Jews, a traitor by nature.

The two months that preceded the trial were spent by the Statistics Section in a sometimes frantic and generally frustrating attempt to strengthen the case against Dreyfus. To the intense annoyance of the minister, General Mercier, the in-house expert employed by the Banque de France whom the Ministry consulted gave as his opinion that despite the similarities in handwriting the bordereau could have been written by someone other than Dreyfus. Alphonse Bertillon, chief of the Identification Department of the Judicial Police, whose opinion was also sought, propounded an elaborate theory of self-forgery to explain dissimilarities between the handwritings, which were both Dreyfus's: Dreyfus, he held, had altered his handwriting on purpose, copying in certain instances the handwriting of others. Of the three additional experts also consulted, all qualified to give testimony before courts, two declared that the handwriting was Dreyfus's and one that it was not. Mercier was so pleased with Bertillon's work that he arranged for him to explain his system to Jean Casimir-Perier, the president of the republic. After the visit, Casimir-Perier confided to Paléologue that this expert was not simply bizarre, he was mad: a fugitive from an insane asylum.[4] It is difficult to believe that the president, holding that view, would have remained passive if the life of a non-Jewish officer had been at stake. The dissenting views of the Banque de France expert and of one of the experts retained subsequently did not give Mercier pause. He became convinced that Dreyfus was guilty within days after receiving du Paty's report, and his conviction remained unshakeable.

Mercier's decision to prosecute Dreyfus was not universally welcomed in the highest echelons of the government and the army. As military governor of Paris and vice president of the Conseil supérieur de guerre, General Félix Saussier was the highest-ranking French army officer. He deplored the effect on the army of accusing an officer of treason and had doubts about Dreyfus's guilt. Nevertheless, when his approval was required for the prosecution to go forward, he signed the necessary papers. Again according to Paléologue, Saussier subsequently shared with Casimir-Perier his view that Dreyfus was not guilty; Mercier had once again shot himself in the foot. When asked by the president why, in that case, he had issued the order sending Dreyfus before the court-martial, he replied that the report on the investigation had left him no alternative, and besides it didn't matter—the military judges who heard the case would decide it fairly and justly. Saussier had previously advised Mercier that it might be wiser to send Dreyfus to Africa, where the French army was engaged in frequent skirmishes with hostile tribes, in the hope that he would be killed there. The minister's retort was that he would more likely come back with a promotion. Gabriel Hanotaux, the minister of foreign affairs, was also opposed to the prosecution. He feared the diplomatic consequences of revealing that an agent of the Statistics Section had been stealing documents from the German embassy and publicizing the fact that Schwartzkoppen, a

German Imperial Guard officer and an accredited diplomat, was engaged in spying. Hanotaux's concerns were so strong that, at his insistence, the prime minister, Charles Dupuy, likewise of two minds about the case, made Mercier promise not to proceed with the case unless additional proof of guilt were obtained.

The promise proved difficult to keep. No other incriminating evidence was found. Moreover, Dreyfus was a most unlikely spy or traitor. He was rich; he was happily married and had two small children; he had no debts and no vices; he was a graduate of two elite institutions, the Ecole polytechnique and the Ecole supérieure de guerre (the French army's equivalent to the U.S. Army War College); and he had graduated from the latter institution near enough to the top of his class to obtain the prized trainee position at the General Staff. Nothing stood in the way of his becoming in due course a general. Why would such a man peddle secret documents to the German attaché? Only one answer could be given: he was a Jew.

Dreyfus was held incommunicado in the rue du Cherche-midi jail for two weeks, not allowed to enter into contact with his wife or a lawyer. His apartment was searched repeatedly. Under French law, the searches were illegal, and du Paty, whom Mercier put in charge of the preliminary secret investigation, threatened Dreyfus's wife, Lucie, with the direst consequences for her husband if she breathed a word to anyone about either the searches or her husband's imprisonment. Two weeks passed before Dreyfus was shown the bordereau; during that time du Paty had subjected him to six long, verbally brutal interrogations. Du Paty's goal was to obtain a confession by a mixture of threats and offers of leniency. In his unpublished reminiscences Dreyfus wrote that du Paty arrived always in the evening, very late, accompanied by the archivist Gribelin, who acted as his secretary. Du Paty would dictate to Dreyfus bits of text taken from the bordereau, flash words or parts of words taken from the text before his eyes, asking whether he recognized his own handwriting, make veiled allusions to facts that Dreyfus did not understand, and exit with theatrical flair. "If my brain did not fail," Dreyfus wrote, "during those interminable days and nights it was not du Paty's fault. He would leave me to struggle in the void."[5] Dreyfus's only response was to proclaim his innocence. His agitation was such that the commander of the prison, Major Ferdinand Forzinetti, feared for his life and forbade more fanciful methods of questioning that du Paty would have liked to test, such as waking Dreyfus in the middle of the night and shining the light of a powerful flashlight in his eyes. After observing Dreyfus closely during the entire period of his imprisonment, Forzinetti concluded that Dreyfus was innocent, and he became one of the first Dreyfusards who was not a member of the captain's family.

Du Paty, who believed that Dreyfus was guilty, did not hide his frustration from his superiors. During a stormy meeting on October 27 in General de Boisdeffre's office at which Sandherr and Henry were also present, du Paty told Boisdeffre that Dreyfus had not confessed, that the searches of his apartment had produced nothing that incriminated him, and that the only thing that could be used against him was the bordereau. He followed up with a letter to Boisdeffre in which he reiterated his account of Dreyfus's refusal to confess and warned that acquittal was a distinct possibility. In conclusion he suggested that it might be appropriate to stop the proceedings, release Dreyfus, and devise a new plan of action, in the meantime taking steps to prevent him from communicating with agents of foreign powers. The same day, Boisdeffre called du Paty in and told him: "We have gone too far to be able to retreat. Dreyfus is a swine who deserves the firing squad. Get on with your work without worrying about the consequences, and don't sulk."[6] Two days later, du Paty submitted his report to Mercier. In it he called Dreyfus a traitor, but he refrained from making a recommendation about charging him with the crime, leaving it up to the minister to decide on the next step.

Meanwhile, the incarceration of Dreyfus had ceased to be a secret. Leaks to the press had enabled the nationalist anti-Semitic Parisian daily *L'Eclair* to scoop the competition and publish an article on October 31 in its evening edition confirming the rumor that an officer attached to the General Staff had been arrested and charged with treason. Newspapers appearing the next day filled out what was known of the story: the officer was Alfred Dreyfus, an artillery officer, thirty-five years old, with an address on avenue du Trocadéro. There were hints that because the officer was Jewish the affair would be covered up through the influence of powerful Jews. Mercier could now expect that if he ordered Dreyfus's release the nationalist anti-Semitic press would excoriate him for botching the investigation and not moving with sufficient vigor against a Jew. On the other hand, if he kept Dreyfus in jail and opened an official investigation, and, as seemed possible, the charges against Dreyfus were subsequently dismissed or he was acquitted, a different sort of scandal would erupt. Mercier would be blamed for having brought frivolous and dishonoring charges against an officer and for foolishly risking a diplomatic crisis with Germany. In addition to the damage to his reputation, a likely consequence would be the loss of his cabinet seat. Mercier was known for his stubbornness and tendency toward impulsive decisions, traits that were exacerbated by his unpopularity at the time and by attacks that had been made on some of his other decisions. On November 7 he launched a formal judicial investigation the consequences of which were so grave that a considerable amount of sleuthing has since been devoted to establishing who was responsible for the leaks to the press that helped precipitate it. Suspicions have centered on Major Henry, as the officer most eager for the prosecution to go forward, but they have never been confirmed, and no culprit has been reliably identified.[7]

The need for incriminating evidence now became even more urgent. Since it could not be found and embarrassment to Mercier had to be avoided, it became necessary to create it. Henry undertook the task. With the assistance of the archivist Gribelin he assembled—and where it seemed useful altered—the components of what became known as the *dossier secret.* Included in it were copies of strikingly indiscreet letters exchanged between Schwartzkoppen and the Italian military attaché, Colonel Alessandro Panizzardi; an almost incomprehensible draft of a memorandum by Schwartzkoppen in which he appears to muse on the advantages and risks of enlisting the services of an unnamed

French officer; three letters from a Spanish military attaché that, as altered and embellished by Henry, alerted his correspondent, an agent of Statistics Section, to the fact that an officer on the General Staff was selling information to the German attaché; and a memorandum of three to four pages, prepared by du Paty, commenting on the documents and giving them the desired slant. The most important letter from Panizzardi to Schwartzkoppen in the dossier, which would continue to reappear and be referred to over the course of the affair, concerned plans of military installations in Nice that "cette canaille de D. [that swine D.] has given me for you." According to Schwartzkoppen, "D."—invariably identified as Dreyfus by his accusers—was in fact a certain Monsieur Dubois, a civilian working for the Cartography Section of the Ministry of War who had for years been selling plans of French military installations to the two attachés.[8]

The preparation of the forgeries in the dossier secret was a crime under French law, as was the use to which they were put in Dreyfus's court-martial. Mercier recognized the danger they posed to himself and his subordinates and following Dreyfus's conviction gave orders that the court-martial file be retained at the Ministry of War rather than in the archives of the army command in Paris. The Dupuy government fell in early January, and before leaving office Mercier burned his personal copy of du Paty's memorandum in Sandherr's presence, ordering him to make sure that no trace of it remained at the Statistics Section. At the same time he returned the other documents constituting the dossier secret, which he had kept in his possession, to Sandherr so that they could be reinserted in the various files from which they had been culled and thus be harder to reassemble. As an added precaution, in a strange ceremony he asked his General Staff accomplices—Boisdeffre, Gonse, Sandherr, Henry, and du Paty—to swear on their honor never to reveal what had happened before or during the Dreyfus trial. But Sandherr had served as chief of the Statistics Section for more than a decade, and out of bureaucratic habit he disobeyed the order to destroy the du Paty memorandum, adding his own copy of the memorandum and photographic copies of the bordereau to the dossier secret and placing the entire package in a sealed envelope in his office. A few months later Sandherr, who was suffering from advanced general paralysis (a late stage of syphilis), which affects cognitive as well as motor functions, was forced to retire for medical reasons. He entrusted the envelope to Picquart, his successor as the chief of the Statistics Section.

Dreyfus's court-martial began on December 19, 1894. Almost immediately, the prosecutor demanded *huis clos,* closing the hearing to all except the prosecutor, the defendant and his counsel, and witnesses. Dreyfus's counsel, Edgar Demange, protested strenuously, having pinned his hopes in large measure on making the public aware of the preposterousness of the charge and the controverted nature of the only proof—the bordereau— that had been adduced against the defendant. The presiding judge overruled him; Demange was allowed to file his pleading and argue the point but only after the other members of the tribunal had withdrawn. However, in violation of the huis clos order and the code of military justice, both Picquart, who had been instructed by Mercier and Boisdeffre to observe the trial and report to them, and the prefect of police were allowed to be present. After two days of testimony by witnesses for the prosecution, the intrinsic weakness of its case remained apparent. The bordereau, with its disputed authorship, was still the only potential proof of guilt. The allegations of witnesses for the prosecution about Dreyfus's past associations with women of questionable virtue, his gambling, his unpleasant personality, and his excessive curiosity, even if true, only blackened his character; they did not make him a traitor.

It was time for the Statistics Section to go on the attack. Henry, who had already testified, asked to be recalled to the witness stand. Interrogated by the president of the tribunal, to whom he had previously fed the questions that should be put to him, Henry stated that an honorable person had warned him ten months earlier, in February, that an officer attached to the Ministry of War was a traitor. In another conversation a month later the same informant had made the charge more specific: the traitor was attached to the Second Department of the General Staff (Dreyfus's posting). After this windup Henry pointed at Dreyfus and exclaimed, "Le traître, le voici!" The accused and his lawyer rose, protesting, and demanded the name of Henry's informant. As sole answer Henry pointed to his French officer's cap and declared: "There are things in an officer's head that even his kepi isn't allowed to know!" This coup de théâtre notwithstanding, that evening Picquart told Mercier that the case was still going badly; the prefect of police similarly reported to President Casimir-Perier that he thought acquittal was likely. In the memoir he published in 1901, *Cinq années de ma vie,* Dreyfus recalled that on December 22, after hearing Demange's closing statement, he was certain that he would be acquitted.[9]

Faced with the likelihood of failure, Mercier decided to play the trump card he had held back. In Sandherr's presence he handed the dossier secret to du Paty and dispatched him to the hearing with instructions to deliver it to the president of the tribunal and say that the general had given him a "moral order as strong as possible" to make the contents of the dossier known to the judges. The submission of documents to the court in secret, without giving Dreyfus and his counsel an opportunity to examine and challenge them, was a crime under the military code of justice and the laws applicable to judicial proceedings other than courts-martial. The documents' impact on the military judges was beyond doubt. Reporting as usual to Boisdeffre and Mercier in the evening, Picquart, at the time convinced of Dreyfus's guilt, told the generals that if he had not known that the judges had the dossier in their possession he would not have been able to remain calm. His serenity was justified: after only an hour of deliberation, during which parts of the dossier were read aloud by the president and parts by another officer, the tribunal unanimously found Dreyfus guilty and condemned him to military degradation and perpetual imprisonment in a fortified enclosure. It was the most severe sentence that could be imposed, the penalty of death for political crimes, including treason, having been abolished by the Constitution of 1848. Two days later, on Christmas Eve, Mercier introduced a bill in the Chamber of Deputies that would have reestablished capital punishment. The bill did not pass.

The degradation ceremony in the courtyard of the Ecole militaire that took place on January 5, 1895, has been described countless times. A gigantic Garde républicaine noncommissioned officer ripped off Dreyfus's insignia of rank, epaulettes, buttons, and braid, and broke his sword on his knee. His uniform in shreds, the convict performed the "Judas parade": flanked by four artillery troopers, he marched along the sides of the immense square courtyard lined by soldiers drawn from each regiment garrisoned in Paris standing at attention; at every opportunity he cried out that he was innocent and proclaimed his love of France; beyond the courtyard, a huge mob, held back with great difficulty by the police, yelled death to the traitor, the Judas, the dirty Jew, in an outpouring of hatred that would thenceforth greet Dreyfus each time he was exposed to the public. Six weeks later, he boarded the vessel that would transport him to Devil's Island.

The false accusation and the miscarriage of justice have passed into legend, so that the barbaric scene and the humiliation of the innocent victim just described make us cringe with sympathy and horror. For the most part contemporaries perceived it differently. The very civilized Paléologue made no bones about instinctively disliking Jews. At the same time he claimed that he was repelled by anti-Semitism, having seen at close range its iniquity and aberrations.[10] These two apparently contradictory positions were far from uncommon in elegant society. Believing that Dreyfus was guilty, Paléologue had donned the uniform of a reserve infantry officer and attended the degradation ceremony as Sandherr's guest along with the Statistics Section officers. He recorded his impressions as follows: "If I had any doubts as to

Dreyfus's guilt at the time of the trial, now I haven't any. In my opinion, his attitude during the degradation parade put the finishing touch on the verdict. In order to submit with docility, with such passivity, to that kind of torture, this man cannot have any moral sensitivity. Not a gesture of rebellion, not a cry of horror, not a tear, not a murmur! It is true that he protested several times that he was innocent. But all his protestations sounded false; one did not sense in them any warmth of soul; one could have said the voice of an automaton."[11] Many of the impressions recorded by nationalist and decidedly anti-Semitic observers of the ceremony were much harsher. A common theme was Dreyfus's inability to express his feelings in the sort of noble and convincing manner that would be second nature for a real Frenchman.

It was a fact that Dreyfus's voice was weak and when he forced it, it had an unpleasantly tinny sound. That he lacked a "command voice" was mentioned in otherwise laudatory reviews by his superiors. But the fact that he sounded strangled was in reality of a piece with his character. The image that emerges from the memoir of his imprisonment on Devil's Island, from the letters he wrote to his wife, Lucie, while imprisoned in the Cherchemidi prison and later on Devil's Island, and from his memoirs is that of a serious and modest man who had nothing heroic about him except obstinate and taciturn courage. He was incapable of eloquence and grand gestures. Nowhere in his writings from Devil's Island is there to be found the "gesture of rebellion" that Paléologue would have wished to see him make during the degradation ceremony. First and foremost, he considered himself a soldier obligated to show both respect for his hierarchical superiors and obedience. He believed in their righteousness.

A special law, inspired by General Mercier with Dreyfus in mind and enacted without debate by the French legislature, had been required to make possible his deportation to Devil's Island. Under prior law, in effect since 1872, as a political prisoner (a category that included prisoners convicted of treason) Dreyfus could have been deported only to Ducos Island, off New Caledonia, where deportees' wives and children were allowed to join them. Dreyfus's place of incarceration and the regime to which he was subjected, both designed by Mercier, made this impossible. Devil's Island, the smallest of the three Salvation Islands, situated some six nautical miles off the coast of French Guiana, is an arid rocky formation measuring less than one square mile with only a few coconut trees growing on it. It had previously been a leper colony, but the lepers were gone, and their huts had been burned down to prepare for Dreyfus's arrival. The largest of the three islands, Ile royale, served as the seat of the prison administration. Ile Saint-Joseph, the middle island, was a prison for handicapped or insane convicts. The climate of all three Salvation Islands was so harsh and malarial that deportation there had long been considered tantamount to a death sentence. Indeed, soon after arriving on the island Dreyfus began to suffer from severe attacks of malaria.

He was lodged in a newly constructed twelve-foot-by-twelve -foot stone cell with two barred windows and a single door with openings that gave anyone looking in an unobstructed view of the cell's interior. The door led out to a smaller room, in which an armed guard, relieved every two hours, kept watch round the clock. The iron door that led to the outside clanged when the guards came in and went out, making unbroken sleep impossible. The population of the island consisted of Dreyfus and the guards; they were forbidden to speak to him and he to them. The rule of silence was strictly enforced during the entire period of his imprisonment, from the spring of 1895 until the summer of 1899; it applied with equal rigor when Dreyfus was confined to his cell and during recreation when, followed by an armed guard, he was allowed to move around outside the hut in a bare space that offered no shade from the tropical sun. The only persons Dreyfus spoke to were the head guard, the military physician who came from Ile royale when summoned by the guards, and the director of the Salvation Island prisons on his inspection visits. Daytime temperature often exceeded 105 degrees, but Dreyfus had no means of taking a shower to cool himself off. The military physician had recommended that he be allowed to bathe in the sea, but the prison administration refused permission. His rations were supposed to be those of a soldier, but without wine. In practice this meant that in the morning he was given lard or a piece of raw meat, dried beans, and green coffee beans. He cooked his meals on a fire, which he was allowed to make in his cell with wood he gathered during recreation periods. As he was not given a plate or a pot, he fashioned implements from tin cans. Deportees were allowed to buy canned food with their own money, but various administrative obstacles were put in his way, and the efforts of his brother Mathieu to organize a regular supply of provisions from Cayenne, on the mainland of French Guiana, were likewise frustrated by the prison administration. Humiliating random body searches were frequent.

Dreyfus was authorized to write and receive letters, but those he wrote were redacted by Ministry of Colonies censors to delete all specific references to the conditions of his imprisonment. From letters addressed to him, censors deleted news about the outside world, including references to the efforts being made by his wife and Mathieu, along with a growing group of Dreyfusards, to obtain his freedom and exoneration. Halfway through Dreyfus's imprisonment, censors began to copy the correspondence and, keeping the originals in the ministry files, sent copies to the addressees. Their purpose was to prevent originals, on which secret messages about plans to escape and the like might have been written in disappearing ink, from reaching the addressee.

No one had access to the island without the specific permission of the director of prisons on the Salvation Islands. The military physician could treat Dreyfus only in his cell; removal to the military hospital on Ile royale was forbidden. Dreyfus was allowed to have books and pen and paper. However, he had no lamp, so that even though a small light was kept burning in his cell all night so that the guard could watch him, once night fell he was unable to read.

The law had been changed in order to make it possible to send Dreyfus to Devil's Island. That change, however, did not affect the other provisions of existing law regulating the treatment of deportees. According to the standard French legal commentary, deportation consisted of transportation to a distant colony that the deportee was not allowed to leave. Within the colony, however, the detainee's freedom was to be restricted only to the extent necessary to maintain order and prevent escape. Incarceration in cells was not authorized. The punitive regime devised for Dreyfus, and rigorously enforced by two successive ministers of colonies, thus constituted an abuse of power and violation of the law. It reflected General Mercier's desire to punish Dreyfus for his obduracy: unwillingness to provide a confession that would erase all doubts about his guilt. On Mercier's orders, du Paty had resorted to threats and blandishments to obtain one, both before the trial and afterward, while Dreyfus was still imprisoned in Paris, but Dreyfus had remained steadfast in his refusal. It is not unlikely that the conditions of his deportation would have been less harsh—perhaps he would have been sent to Ducos Island, as du Paty apparently had hinted—if he had not defied the general.

In September 1896, an article in an English newspaper foolishly planted by a journalist Mathieu had charged with the mission of keeping the case from being forgotten by the public announced without any foundation that Dreyfus had escaped. The news spread to France and provoked an outcry against the government's laxity. The rumor was promptly denied, but the consequences for Dreyfus were grave. During the two months that followed, he was shackled at night to a metal bed by twin iron buckles placed over his ankles. Unable to move, he was tormented by the mosquitoes, biting ants, and spider crabs that swarmed in the cell, as well as by the unbearable heat. Although he tried to protect himself by stuffing pieces of cloth between the shackles and his flesh, suppurating sores formed on his ankles and did not heal. The journal of his captivity, being a nineteenth-century document, says nothing about how he relieved himself, but we can imagine the unspeakable details. The security of his cell was reinforced by a double palisade. During the construction period of some two and a half months he was confined to the cell day and night, a procedure that was later repeated each time work details arrived on the island for any purpose. The new fence was eight feet high and stood so close to the cell windows that it obstructed the passage of both light and air. The exterior palisade left a space—within which Dreyfus was allowed to walk during the day—that was patrolled day and night by an armed guard whose duty was to assist the guard stationed inside the hut.

As one would expect, Dreyfus's health deteriorated. In addition to malaria and sores on his ankles, he suffered from dysentery, constant insomnia, infected insect bites, attacks of a fever apparently not related to malaria the cause of which was never determined, and a condition the military physician diagnosed as cerebral congestion. Except in moments of blackest despair, he fought hard to keep his mind focused: he studied English, translated passages from Shakespeare into French, and reconstructed from memory elements of integral and differential calculus. Notwithstanding these efforts, the military physician who examined him in April 1897 declared that solitary confinement and obligatory silence—which by then had lasted two years and was to continue until Dreyfus left Devil's Island for France in the summer of 1899—had caused him to experience difficulty in articulating and forming sentences. Another doctor, also summoned by the government, examined Dreyfus in September 1899. His report concluded that Dreyfus was a finished man.

Meanwhile, l'Affaire Dreyfus was tearing France apart. By 1898 the Dreyfusard camp, led by Mathieu Dreyfus, included centrist and left-wing politicians, and, with significant and notorious exceptions, most leading intellectuals, artists, writers, and academics, as well as, in smaller numbers, army officers and members of the clergy. Initially, the absence of a motive for the crime stood out among the aspects of the case that convinced adherents of Dreyfus's innocence. Later came revelations of the illegalities committed at the Paris court-martial. Public opinion outside of France was overwhelmingly on the side of Dreyfus: French anti-Dreyfusards were ridiculed in the press, in public meetings, and often most painfully in private conversations. Spectacular supporters of Dreyfus outside France included Queen Victoria and her attorney general; Empress Eugénie, the widow of Napoleon III; the Bourbon, Orléans, and Bonaparte pretenders to the French throne; Prince Albert of Monaco; the great explorer Henry Morton Stanley and his wife; Mark Twain; and, according to some, the pope and leading Vatican prelates. Anti-Dreyfusards were a right-wing coalition of army officers, anti-Semites, militarists, extreme nationalists, anti-republicans of every stripe, royalists and Bonapartists oblivious of the views of their princes, members of conservative bourgeoisie and provincial nobility, clericalists, and lower ranks of the clergy.

It was an article of faith for Dreyfusards that the man on Devil's Island must be given the opportunity to prove his innocence at a fair trial, even at the cost of exposing the foolish, as well as criminal, machinations of the army's General Staff and at least two ministers of war. Indeed, from the left-wing point of view, such exposure was to be desired: it would loosen the grip on the army of aristocratic, anti-republican officers and their Jesuit mentors. For anti-Dreyfusards, on the contrary, the overriding first duty was to save the honor of the army and its chiefs, and to stand behind the men responsible for the defense of the nation. If the price of restoring the liberty and good name of an Alfred Dreyfus was the humiliation of a General Mercier or a General de Boisdeffre, it was too high. Reasons of state precluded its payment. It was better to let Dreyfus rot on Devil's Island.

As for Dreyfus, all through the years of his imprisonment he remained naively or sublimely confident in the army. Unaware of the struggle of his partisans to free him and the malefactions of the General Staff, he was convinced that Generals Mercier and de Boisdeffre, as well as his other chiefs, were making efforts to find the real traitor. There is no mention in his prison memoir of anti-Semitism or his own Jewishness, although before the deportation he could not have helped being aware of the corrosive hatred swirling about him in France. Clearly, he was not willing to think that his being a Jew was relevant to his case or his status, which, he persisted in believing with the stubbornness of delusion, was that of a Frenchman and a French officer. And after his return from Devil's Island, he refused to join those of his Dreyfusard supporters who had sought to politicize his case by attacking the army. His fervent desire was to have his good name restored by the institutions he loved and had served: the army and the French Republic. Léon Blum, the great socialist and future prime minister of France, who had been as a young man an early and passionate Dreyfusard, gave voice to the fundamental perception that has clouded Dreyfus's image: "Really, he had no affinity with his 'affair,' no vocation for the role which a caprice of History forced upon him. If he hadn't been Dreyfus, would he have even been a 'Dreyfusard'?"[12]

After a long struggle, French political and judicial processes were made to function as intended. In the summer of 1906, when the Cour de Cassation (Court of Cassation, France's highest court for matters governed by civil and criminal law, as opposed to military or administrative law), reversing the Rennes court-martial that had retried Dreyfus in 1899 and found him guilty with extenuating circumstances, rendered its judgment declaring Dreyfus innocent of any crime, its decision was greeted by the public with a calm that bordered on indifference. He was reintegrated into the army with the rank of major and made a chevalier of the Legion of Honor. The abuses of power and crimes committed by General Mercier and his General Staff co-conspirators had been fully exposed, but an amnesty law voted by the French legislature in 1900 had given them immunity from prosecution.

The tragedy of September 11, 2001, was followed by an international outpouring of sympathy for the United States and a willingness to stand by it in the struggle against terrorism that became known as the war on terror. Unfortunately, the subsequent actions of President George W. Bush, both at home and abroad, brought opprobrium upon the United States, alienating traditional allies. One cause of the anger was the administration's ill-considered Iraq adventure. The other was the army's mistreatment of detainees, the overwhelming majority of whom were captured in Afghanistan and Iraq, an action that has remade the image of the United States into that of a land where torture is an instrument of government policy. The prison complex at the Guantánamo Naval Base in Cuba, which opened in 2002, became the symbol of U.S. brutality and arbitrariness. During his presidential campaign, Barack Obama pledged that he would close Guantánamo and make respect for the Constitution and the principles on which the United States was founded the lodestar of his government. There is no reason to doubt his resolve.

The photographs showing the abuse of prisoners in the Abu Ghraib jail operated by the U.S. military in Iraq are notorious. Torture has likewise been practiced at Bagram Air Base in Afghanistan, perhaps at other facilities in Iraq, and in the CIA's secret jails outside the United States. According to International Red Cross and FBI reports as well as other evidence that came to light in 2008, detainees have been tortured at Guantánamo as well. A report by Physicians for Human Rights describes this torture: it has included beatings, sexual assaults (including the case of a man who was sodomized with a broomstick), electric shock, sexual and other forms of humiliation, sleep deprivation, and outlandish threats. As the Executive Summary to the Senate Armed Services Committee's inquiry into the treatment of detainees in U.S. custody put it, "The abuse of detainees . . . cannot simply be attributed to he actions of 'a few bad apples' acting on their own. The fact is that senior officials in the United States Government solicited information on how to use aggressive techniques, redefined the law to create the appearance of their legality, and authorized their use against detainees." The "senior officials" included the vice president, the secretaries of state and defense, and the national security adviser, who had all involved themselves in choreographing torture sessions—euphemistically referred to as "aggressive" or "enhanced" interrogation—from the White House. Vice President Cheney publicly admitted that he had "signed off" on the water boarding (immobilizing a prisoner on a surface inclined downward and repeatedly pouring water over his face to induce a state analogous to drowning) of three detainees, Khalid Sheikh Mohammed, Abu Zurbaydah, and Al Nashim; he said he didn't consider it torture.[13]

The government's redefining of the law appeared in opinions and memoranda prepared by top officials of the U.S. Justice Department condoning torture and reinterpreting the international obligations of the United States. These reinterpretations later had to be withdrawn, but "aggressive" methods of interrogation continued to be sanctioned by the administration. As recently as the fall of 2007, Attorney General Michael Mukasey professed not to know whether water boarding was a form of torture. CIA tapes of torture sessions have apparently been destroyed, but while they existed interrogators, physicians, and psychologists were flown to Thailand to study them and profit from their colleagues' experience. As Jane Mayer reported in *The Dark Side: The Inside Story of How the War on Terror Has Turned into a War on American Ideals,* published in July 2008, one of the contributions of psychologists was to assist the CIA in instilling "learned helplessness"—the loss of willpower and all sense of control—in prisoners, as well as total dependence on their captors, by repeated traumas. By perverting medicine and psychology in the service of torture, the United States has followed in the steps of Nazi Germany and Soviet Russia. The Department of Foreign Affairs of Canada, America's nearest ally, put the United States on the list of countries that torture or abuse prisoners, along with Afghanistan, Israel, China, Egypt, Iran, Mexico, Saudi Arabia, and Syria. After protests by the United States, the foreign minister of Canada announced that the list would be "reviewed and rewritten," a commitment that could not take away the sting of the department's first judgment. In July 2008 the select Foreign Affairs Committee of the U.K. House of Commons concluded that Great Britain could no longer rely on U.S. assurances that America did not use torture.[14]

A grim insight into the operation of the United States' own Devil's Island in Guantánamo became available in November 2007 with the publication on the Internet of "Camp Delta Standard Operating Procedures (SOP)." Several hundred pages long, the SOP is an eerie echo of the "Instructions for Deportation Administration of Devil's Island" that had governed the conditions of Dreyfus's imprisonment. Both provide for solitary confinement (at Camp Delta in the maximum security unit and in the brig for defined periods of time, on Devil's Island in Dreyfus's cell in perpetuity), and the two have analogous restrictions on access, recreation, correspondence, and rations, as well as analogous tedious instructions to the guards. Dreyfus was shackled to a metal cot at night for eight weeks. Shackles—the "three-piece suit" consisting of leg irons, handcuffs, a chain worn around the waist as a belt, and two chains that connect the leg irons and handcuffs to the chain belt—are constants at Guantánamo whenever prisoners leave their cells, especially when they are on their way to and from an "interrogation booth," where the shackles are attached to a ring fixed in the cement floor. The SOP sheds no light on what transpires in the interrogation booths; that is left to the reader's imagination.[15]

On December 22, 2008, the Brookings Institution, a respected think tank, published "The Current Detainee Population of Guantánamo: An Empirical Study." According to the report, since the camp's 2002 opening 779 detainees have passed through Guantánamo, comprising all detainees captured in Afghanistan and Iraq, and all those kidnapped by the CIA who had been held in secret prisons and subsequently transferred to the naval base in Cuba. All these detainees had been designated "enemy combatants" by President Bush, an elastic concept defined in a Department of Defense order signed by Deputy Secretary of Defense Paul Wolfowitz as including "any person who has committed a belligerent act or has directly supported hostilities in aid of enemy armed forces." Out of 558 detainees present at the base on the date of the Wolfowitz order, 330 have been transferred or released, leaving 248 detainees at Guantánamo as of December 16, 2008. The destination of the detainees who have been transferred is unknown. Of the remaining group, 60 have been "cleared for release, their departure being subject to negotiations with other countries." Based on the report, that would seem to leave 188 detainees at the base as of the end of 2008 who might still be charged with crimes or quietly let go.[16]

The first step on the road to a detainee's release has been to challenge his designation as an enemy combatant. The Wolfowitz order established a forum for that purpose, the Combatant Status Review Tribunals (CSRTs), in response to the rising concern about the legality of the detainees' incarceration and to a comment by Justice Sandra Day O'Connor in the Supreme Court case *Hamdi v. Rumsfeld* (2004) to the effect that the requirements of constitutional due process might be satisfied by appropriately constituted military tribunals even if these did not provide the same procedures and protections offered by civilian criminal courts. The same day as the *Hamdi* decision, however, June 28, 2004, in what became a four-year tug of war over detainees' rights between the Bush administration and the Supreme Court, the Court held in *Rasul v. Bush* that Guantánamo detainees were entitled to challenge the legality of their incarceration by a writ of habeas corpus filed in a federal district court. *Rasul* opened the way for Lakhdar Boumediene, a thirty-six-year-old Algerian detainee, and others to challenge the legality of their detentions by petitioning in a federal district court for the writ of habeas corpus. In response, Congress attempted to overturn *Rasul* by passing the Detainee Treatment Act (DTA, 2005), which made the Circuit Court of Appeals for the District of Columbia the sole court empowered to undertake (very limited) review of decisions of the CSRTs, as well as military commissions established pursuant to Military Commission Order No. 1, dated August 31, 2005.

The next confrontation between the administration and the Supreme Court was the Pentagon's attempt to prosecute Salim Ahmed Hamdan, a Guantánamo detainee, for war crimes before a military commission convened by the president. Relying on

Rasul, Hamdan conceded the authority of the United States to detain him as an enemy combatant but successfully challenged by a writ of habeas corpus the legality of the military commission that was to try him for war crimes. In the case that bears his name, *Hamdan v. Rumsfeld* (2006), the Supreme Court brushed aside the Pentagon's contention that the Court's jurisdiction had been ousted by the DTA, and interpreted the jurisdiction-stripping provision as inapplicable to a habeas corpus proceeding that, like Hamdan's, had begun before the passage of the act. The Court went on to hold that the military commission established by the president lacked the power to try Hamdan because its structure and procedures violated both the Uniform Code of Military Justice and the four Geneva Conventions signed by the United States in 1949. Among the procedural defects singled out by the Court were the inability of the accused and his civilian counsel to find out what evidence was being presented during any part of the proceeding that the presiding officer decided to close to them; the admissibility of any evidence that in the presiding officer's estimation would have value to a reasonable person even if it was hearsay or obtained by coercion; and the power of the presiding officer to deny the accused and his civilian counsel access to classified and other "protected" information that the presiding officer had concluded was probative. The analogy with Dreyfus is irresistible: he too was tried by a tribunal dominated by his accusers, and he too was convicted on the basis of secret evidence that neither he nor his counsel had an opportunity to challenge or even knew about. So is another memory: that of the dogged persistence of the French Court of Cassation (as noted, the Cour de Cassation, the French equivalent of the U.S. Supreme Court for all matters outside the administrative and military law systems) in its review of the iniquitous verdicts of the Paris and Rennes military tribunals that eventually led to their being overturned.

Under extreme pressure by the Bush administration to counter the effects of *Hamdan,* Congress enacted the Military Commissions Act (MCA) of 2006, establishing military commissions with marginally improved protections for defendants. Their decisions were made reviewable on a limited basis only by the District of Columbia Circuit Court, and Congress left no doubt that it intended to preclude applications of Guantánamo detainees for a writ of habeas corpus whenever they were filed. The Supreme Court responded to this new and audacious attempt to put Guantánamo beyond the reach of the law in *Boumediene v. Bush,* decided June 12, 2008. The petitioners were Boumediene and other native Algerians residing in Bosnia and Herzegovina who had acquired Bosnian citizenship or permanent resident status. They were arrested by Bosnian authorities in October 2001 because of their alleged involvement in a plot to bomb the U.S. embassy in Sarajevo. Upon their release from prison in Sarajevo on January 17, 2002, they were seized by Bosnian and U.S. personnel and transported to Guantánamo, where they had been incarcerated ever since. They filed petitions for a writ of habeas corpus in the District Court for the District of Columbia, which denied them on the ground that Guantánamo detainees had no rights that could be vindicated in a habeas corpus proceeding, and the Court of Appeals for the District of Columbia affirmed the denial. The Supreme Court granted certiorari and overruled the Court of Appeals, holding that the U.S. Constitution had full effect in Guantánamo; that the provision of the Military Commissions Act attempting to deprive the Court of jurisdiction was unconstitutional; and that the writ of habeas corpus was available to aliens detained in Guantánamo since the United States exercised full control over the base even though it was not located in U.S. territory. The only way the courts' jurisdiction could be superseded, the Court continued, was by an act of Congress framed in conformity with the Suspension Clause of the Constitution. Neither side had argued that such a suspension had taken place. Proceeding from there, the Court held that because the procedures provided the DTA and the MCA for reviewing the petitioners' detainee status were not an adequate substitute for review under the writ of habeas corpus, the MCA operated as an unconstitutional suspension of that writ. The stage was thus set for the petitioners to seek relief in a U.S. federal district court. As it turned out, five of the detainees were released by the district court since the allegation that they had planned to travel to Afghanistan to fight against the United States—the predicate for their designation as enemy combatants—had no support other than hearsay testimony by a Guantánamo detainee obtained from an unnamed source, evidence the court held to be insufficient. The petition of the sixth detainee, Belkacem Bensayah, was denied because in his case the government had also alleged that he was an Al Qaeda facilitator who had intended to take up arms against the United States in Afghanistan and to arrange for other combatants to travel there and elsewhere for this purpose. The court ruled that the government's burden of proof had been met with respect to those allegations.

Among the 188 (according to the Brookings report) detainees now at Guantánamo who have not been cleared for release there are surely many who have been designated enemy combatants with no greater justification than that used against the Algerians. They are there by mistake or because they were sold to the CIA or the U.S. military in Afghanistan or Pakistan by bounty hunters. In all probability they represent no greater threat to the United States than the average man in the street anywhere in the Middle East. A case in point is the detention of Sami al-Haj, a former cameraman for the Arabic news network Al-Jazeera whose cause was taken up by the Committee to Protect Journalists. Al-Haj had been seized by Pakistani intelligence in December 2001 while traveling near the Afghanistan border, even though he held a valid visa to work for Al-Jazeera in Afghanistan. In January 2002 he was handed over to the U.S. military, which dispatched him to Guantánamo. After six years' detention, during which he was never charged, he was released on May 1, 2008, and sent to his native Sudan without any sort of proceeding, simply as a result of political pressure exerted on his behalf.[17]

In the wake of *Boumediene,* more detainees will doubtless be released through writs of habeas corpus. This is already happening in the case of Mohammed el Gharani, a citizen of Chad who was arrested by authorities in Pakistan in the fall of 2001 (when he was fourteen years old), turned over to U.S. forces in early 2002, and dispatched to Guantánamo, where he has been imprisoned ever since. The designation of this child prisoner as an enemy combatant was based on allegations that he had stayed at an Al Qaeda–affiliated guesthouse in Afghanistan, received military training at an Al Qaeda–affiliated camp, served as a courier for several high-ranking Al Qaeda members, fought against U.S. forces in the Battle of Tora Bora, and was a member of an Al Qaeda cell in London. El Gharani denied these allegations, explaining that he had gone to Pakistan to escape the prejudice against Chadians in Saudi Arabia, where he had lived previously, and to learn computer and English-language skills in order to make a better life for himself. The district court judge, constrained in writing his opinion by the classified nature of the government's proof, held that the proof submitted to him was insufficient, being nothing more than the factually inconsistent declarations of two other detainees, whose credibility the government itself characterized as undetermined or questionable. Granting el Gharani's petition for a writ of habeas corpus, the court directed the government to take all necessary steps to facilitate his release.[18]

As of the end of 2007, only one Guantánamo prisoner had been tried and convicted by a military commission. That was David Hicks, an Australian citizen who pleaded guilty in accordance with a deal brokered by the Australian government that ensured his release. In return for being able to leave Guantánamo and serve a light sentence in Australia, Hicks was obliged to declare that he had not been mistreated while in captivity, to agree to refrain from speaking to the media for one year, and to pledge not to sue the United States for the mistreatment he had suffered.

In August 2008 the government once more brought Salim Ahmed Hamdan, the successful petitioner in *Hamdan v. Rumsfeld*, to trial for war crimes before a military commission. Hamdan, a fortyish Yemeni with a fourth-grade education, had been Osama bin Laden's driver and bodyguard. In the 2006 proceedings, he had conceded that the United States was entitled to detain him as an enemy combatant. The war crimes of which he stood accused before the 2008 military commission were conspiring to engage in terrorist acts and provide surface-to-air missiles to Al Qaeda and providing Al Qaeda with material support. The jury of military officers convicted him of providing material support and acquitted him of the conspiracy charge. It imposed a jail sentence of sixty months—but only after having first received assurance from the judge that the time Hamdan had spent as a detainee in Guantánamo would reduce the time he would have to spend in jail. Since Hamdan had been detained for five and a half years, the resulting net sentence was approximately five months. That it took so long to bring this small cog in bin Laden's machine to trial and convict him, and that it was only the second conviction of a Guantánamo detainee, put on display the tragic absurdity of the claim the Bush administration used to justify the scandal of its detention system, namely, that only the most dangerous terrorists were incarcerated at Guantánamo. Hamdan served out his sentence, was returned to Yemen, and was released there in the first week of January 2009, to live with his family.[19]

The press was excluded from much of Hamdan's 2008 trial, a ruling by the military judge that recalls the huis clos imposed in

Dreyfus's 1894 Paris court-martial. There is another echo. The jury of army officers found Dreyfus guilty "with extenuating circumstances" at the conclusion of Dreyfus's second court-martial in Rennes. A day later these same officers addressed a request to the president of the republic that Dreyfus be spared a second military degradation. Presumably they were overcome by pity and perhaps shame when they reflected on what they had done. It does not seem unlikely that the army officers who served as Hamdan's jury held their noses when they voted to convict him of the crime of driving bin Laden's car.

In decision after decision the Supreme Court rebuffed the Bush administration's attempts to place its dragnet detentions beyond the purview of the Constitution. The coup de grâce may have been administered to the Pentagon's penitentiary system by one of its own, Susan J. Crawford, a retired military judge who, as the "convening authority," was the administration's top official in charge of the military commission trials on the base. (Previously she had been general counsel for the army during the Reagan administration and inspector general of the Pentagon when Vice President Cheney was secretary of defense under President George H. W. Bush.) In May 2008 she dismissed the charges, without comment and without prejudice—meaning that as a legal matter they could be reinstated—against Mohammed al-Qahtani, one of six detainees charged with masterminding the September 11th attacks. She approved putting the other five on trial and seeking the death penalty. Crawford explained her reasons for not allowing Qahtani to stand trial in an interview with Bob Woodward of the *Washington Post* in January 2009. "We tortured [Mohammed al-]Qahtani," she said, citing the nature of the interrogation techniques, their duration, and the impact on Qahtani's health. "The techniques [the interrogators] used were all authorized, but the manner in which they applied them was overly aggressive and too persistent." She gave specifics: "For 160 days his only contact was with the interrogators. . . . Forty-eight of 54 consecutive days of 18- to 20-hour interrogations. Standing naked in front of a female agent. Subject to strip searches. And insults to his mother and sisters." Qahtani was " 'forced to wear a woman's bra and had a thong placed on his head during the course of his interrogation.' With a leash tied to his chains, he was led around the room and 'forced to perform a series of dog tricks.' " All aspects of these interrogations were recorded in minute detail in logs maintained by the military authorities. Judge Crawford believed that Qahtani was the missing twentieth hijacker, but as far as she was concerned the treatment he had suffered meant he could never be tried, and she was determined to stop any attempt to do so.[20]

The Woodward interview has had great resonance because of the explosive subject matter, the distinguished service record of Judge Crawford, and the eminence and prestige of both Woodward and the *Washington Post*. An even more terrifying window on the abuse of detainees was opened by an interview with Chris Arendt, who had been for two months a guard at the Guantánamo prison. It aired on the BBC World News Service on January 9, 2009. Arendt, who was then nineteen, described abuse that he unhesitatingly called torture: forceful removal of detainees from their cells; kicking them in the face and other blows;

subjecting them to the "frequent flyer program," which calls for a detainee to be moved from one cell to another to prevent him from sleeping, and which in some cases was practiced for as long as two months. Arendt spoke of his fellow guards, for some of whom torture was just a job, while for others—the "psychotic" ones—it was a vacation, the one chance to do things to people that they had always dreamed of.[21]

A month before these interviews, an event occurred that could serve as the farcical epitaph for Guantánamo and the foolish, disastrous endeavor it symbolizes. The five alleged September 11th masterminds, whose trial Judge Crawford had permitted to proceed, found a way to stop it in its tracks. On December 8, 2008, they told the military judge that they wanted to confess in full, a move that challenged the army to put them to death without further ado. As they had surely anticipated, the judge began to ask questions about the procedure to be followed in such cases. Thereupon some of the five suggested that they would change their plea unless he assured them that they would be executed. As Khalid Sheikh Mohammed explained, "We don't want to waste our time with motions." If the detainees were seeking to make the prosecution ridiculous, they succeeded: the court session, attended by reporters from the Arab world, Spain, Brazil, Japan, and elsewhere, disintegrated into legal wrangling about whether the death penalty could be applied based on a guilty plea as opposed to a finding of guilt by a jury of officers; the competence of two detainees to make decisions for themselves, an issue that the judge said would take a substantial period of time to resolve;

and the position taken by the three "competent" detainees to wait to enter a plea "until a decision is made about our brothers."[22]

Perhaps because the Guantánamo detainees have been so numerous, perhaps because they are not American, or perhaps because based on what little is known about them they have seemed unattractive, neither the possibility that their detention was unjustified nor the abuse to which they were subjected has provoked a large part of the American population to anger or outrage. A Quinnipiac University survey conducted days after Barack Obama's election found that although he had pledged repeatedly during the campaign to close Guantánamo, 44 percent of respondents did not want him to, 29 percent thought that he should, and 27 percent were undecided. The comment of the director of the Quinnipiac Polling Institute was that "it's not all smooth sailing for the President-elect. Closing the Guantánamo Bay prison comes up negative."[23] The public presumably has found it easy to believe that anyone held at Guantánamo must be there for a good reason. Just as at the outset of the Dreyfus Affair the French found it easy to believe that Dreyfus must be a traitor because he was a Jew, many Americans had had no trouble believing that the detainees at Guantánamo—and those held in CIA jails—were terrorists simply because they were Muslims. The mistreatment documented in the Abu Ghraib images was greeted in the United States with outrage and shame, but no such images have come out of Guantánamo, and photographs that have appeared in the press of rows of prisoners on the base in orange jumpsuits have seemed remote, somehow abstract, even when the prisoners are shown hooded, in black goggles, kneeling in neat rows with their hands handcuffed behind their backs. But these abstract, indifferent figures are real men, as real as Dreyfus, who had seemed so loathsome to the mob during the degradation ceremony that thousands pushed to get near enough to him to spit in his face.

The favored targets of oppression and injustice remain the same: outsiders and disliked and distrusted minorities. In their case, guilt is never to be doubted. That was the guiding principle of the officer in Franz Kafka's *In the Penal Colony,* and something akin to it was the Bush administration's a priori position in dealing with detainees captured during the war on terror. It is difficult to believe that the scandalous violations of U.S. and international law would have occurred without such a belief. As each generation confronts the outrages committed in its name, analogies to past outrages become clear, illuminating the present. And so does the need for a response to the question that has been posed time and again without losing its urgency: Will there be in that generation men and women ready to defend human rights, and the dignity of every human life, against abuse wrapped in claims of expediency and reasons of state? Dreyfusards—Emile Zola, Jean Jaurès, and Anatole France, to cite only the best known—and Lieutenant Colonel Georges Picquart, who ultimately became Dreyfus's savior, gave the answer for France at the turn of the nineteenth century. Journalists dedicated to exposing the abuses of the Bush administration, members of the federal judiciary unflinchingly upholding the rule of law, military lawyers who have put their careers at risk by taking a stand against torture and kangaroo trials, and civilian lawyers and law professors of all ages who have devoted thousands of hours without pay as legal defenders of Guantánamo detainees have given the answer for the United States. They have redeemed the honor of the nation.

2. "the past is never dead"

"In America the law is King," Thomas Paine wrote in *Common Sense* (1776), "for as in absolute governments the king is the law, so in free countries the law ought to be king, and there ought to be no other." In the wake of the attacks on the World Trade Center and the Pentagon on September 11, 2001, the Bush administration used its proclaimed global war on terror as a justification for opening alarming fissures in the rule of law in the United States. The erratic and lawless actions of successive French ministers of war and high-ranking officers on the army's General Staff in the course of the Dreyfus Affair can similarly be traced to a defining national trauma: the humiliating defeat suffered by the French army in the Franco-Prussian War of 1870. That trauma, and the efforts that followed to rebuild the army, in large measure explain the vehement, indeed hysterical, response of nationalist politicians and journalists, as well as wide segments of the French public, to the danger of disclosures that would impugn the honor of the army chiefs and potentially expose them to prosecution. In addition, everything related to the affair was further envenomed by a new and virulent form of anti-Semitism that had surged in France since the 1880s. Going beyond the traditional anti-Jewish teachings of Christian churches, it combined calls for an end to the "stranglehold" of Jews on the French economy and their disproportionate influence in French professional, intellectual, and artistic life with theories holding that Jews were an inferior and degenerate race that must be extruded from French life. Anti-Semitic hatred found a natural focal point in the Jew who had been accused of treason and convicted.

"An immense disaster, a peace made of despair, loss of life that nothing compensated, a state without foundations, no army other than that which was leaving the enemy's prisons, two provinces torn away, billions to be paid, the victor's troops garrisoned in one-fourth of the territory, the capital streaming with blood spilled in a civil war, a Europe ice cold or ironic: such were the conditions in which a vanquished France resumed the march toward its destiny." This was Charles de Gaulle's grim assessment of the aftermath of the Franco-Prussian War, a conflict the French army had entered unprepared, although the emperor, Napoleon

III, nephew of Napoleon I, and his government had desired the war and in the end provoked it.[1]

Along with other European powers, France had been surprised by Prussia's decisive victory on July 3, 1866, over the Austrian army at the battle of Königgratz (also known as Sadowa), which had forced Austria to sue for peace. The two countries had been at war over Austria's refusal to give up the controlling influence it exercised in Germany through the German Confederation, a political system established in 1815 by the Congress of Vienna. Within weeks after Königgratz, Austria and Prussia signed the peace treaty of Prague, which abolished the confederation. Thereupon, Prussia absorbed some of the confederation's north German member states and forced the others to enter into a north German confederation, which put Prussia in full charge of the foreign and military affairs of its members. Overnight, Germany had been transformed, and Prussia had vaulted from second-tier-power status into the first rank. Its combined population was now almost as large as that of France (30 million to France's 38 million), and its army, based on universal military service, was much larger than the French military force. The industrial potential of the new Prussia likewise threatened France's dominance on the continent. In the opinion of the French political class, all this had happened while Napoleon III had been dozing. After a reign of more than a quarter century—he had arranged the plebiscite in 1852 that ended the Second Republic of which he was president and put him on the throne as emperor—he was perceived as tired and spent. When the early elections he called in the spring of 1869 failed to gather support for his government, he decided that only a victorious war against Prussia could restore his popularity, thus saving his throne and dynasty. As it happened, Otto von Bismarck, Prussia's minister-president and foreign minister, also wanted a Franco-Prussian war, believing that war fever would beat back separatist stirrings in the newly absorbed German states as well as among the members of the new north German confederation, and perhaps even bring the rich and populous Kingdom of Bavaria into the confederation. It was a war that he thought Prussia would win. Unlike France, Prussia was ready. Its General Staff had planned meticulously for the attack.

Fortuitously, the pretext both Bismarck and Napoleon III needed came in June 1870 with the offer by the Spanish government of the throne, vacant since the overthrow of the Spanish Bourbon dynasty in 1868, to a German Hohenzollern prince. The prince accepted, whereupon France declared that it would not tolerate German influence south of the Pyrenees, and the prince's father promptly withdrew the acceptance. That should have defused the situation, but the French minister of war and the prime minister instructed the French ambassador to demand that the Prussian king Wilhelm I guarantee that if the offer were ever renewed it would be rejected. The king refused firmly but politely in a conversation with the French ambassador and sent Bismarck a cable summarizing what had been said. Bismarck saw his opening: he revised the king's account and transformed it into an insult to France, which he made public on July 13.[2] The French government took the bait and demanded an apology. Unsurprisingly, none was proffered, and on July 19 France declared war.

As the aggressor it forfeited such help as might have been forthcoming from Austria, Denmark, or Italy, support on which the French had counted.

On balance, France should have been able to win the war, or at least fight Prussia to a standstill, notwithstanding the numerical superiority of Prussia's army. Although once it had fully mobilized Prussia would eventually field more than a million soldiers against France's four hundred thousand, the Prussian army was made up of conscripts with no more than three years of service to their credit and reservists, while the French fighting force consisted of seasoned veterans of Crimean, Italian, and Mexican campaigns. The French also had important weaponry advantages: a new and lethal breech-loading rifle, colloquially known as the Chassepot after its inventor, and the first machine gun, the Montigny mitrailleuse. Instead, the French were crushed, for reasons that included, on the Prussian side, the genius of the chief of staff of the army, Helmuth von Moltke; infinitely superior staff work that exploited every logistical advantage; and a tactical doctrine that encouraged field commanders at all levels to improvise in response to fast-developing situations. The French had no plans for the war. Their General Staff was disconnected from the battlefield command of the troops; officers went to the front without maps; the French tactical doctrine, which called for occupying strong positions, digging in, and letting the enemy attack, played to Prussian strengths; and French generals regularly failed to attack when the Prussians were at a disadvantage, to coordinate their moves with one another, or to come to one another's assistance.

Although the French army and French guerrillas—the *franc-tireurs*—continued fierce resistance until a provisional peace treaty was signed at Versailles on February 26, 1871, the war had for all practical purposes been lost on September 1, 1870, on the battlefield of Sedan, where Napoleon III was taken prisoner. A definitive peace treaty was entered into three months after Versailles, on May 10, 1871, in Frankfurt. Its terms were harsh, giving Germany—newly unified as the German Empire on January 2 —Alsace and northern Lorraine, which would remain German until Germany was defeated in World War I, and requiring France to pay Germany five billion francs in reparations, at the time an astronomical sum. German troops were to continue to occupy France until it was paid in full. Compounding French misery and the losses on the battlefield (280,000 dead or wounded against Prussian losses of 165,000) was the proto-Communist uprising of Paris, known as the Paris Commune, which began on March 18. The French army laid siege to the starving city and finally retook it during what became known as the Bloody Week (*la semaine sanglante*), in an assault that began on May 21. In the meantime, among other wanton acts of destruction, the Tuileries palace and the Hôtel de Ville had been burned, and the column on place Vendôme, celebrating the triumphs of Napoleon I, torn down. Atrocities were committed on both sides, the loss of life being estimated at 30,000 communards; that number included at least 20,000 executed after the army entered Paris. Thousands more were imprisoned and deported in the spring of 1872 not to Devil's Island, like Dreyfus, or one of the larger Salvation Islands but to Ducos Island off New Caledonia, where their families were able to join them a year later. One of the generals commanding the French army, and personally responsible for the brutality of the repression and the executions that followed, was Gaston de Galliffet. At the time of Dreyfus's second court-martial in Rennes, he held the office of minister of war.

Bearing a major responsibility for the defeat at Sedan, and later for surrendering to the Prussians with his entire army at Metz, where he was occupying an almost impregnable position, was the immensely popular and admired French marshal Achille Bazaine. His bizarre behavior and lethargy during the war and the communications between him and the Prussian command before his surrender were such that in 1873, upon his release from Prussian captivity, he was accused of treason. The court-martial found him guilty and sentenced him to death. Several other high-ranking officers were also tried before military tribunals as traitors. One of Bazaine's fellow marshals, Patrice Mac-Mahon, who had been the commander at Sedan and was now the head of the French state, could not bring himself to give the order to have Bazaine shot. Instead, he commuted the sentence to twenty years' imprisonment, without the military degradation that Dreyfus was to suffer. Not much time passed before Bazaine escaped, probably with the connivance of his military jailers, and he reached Spain, where he lived in great comfort until his death in 1888. In one of the many ironic twists in the Dreyfus Affair, General Mercier, as he was leaving office, took the trouble to inform General Saussier, the army's most senior commander, that the files pertaining to the Dreyfus court-martial would be kept at the Ministry of War, rather than at the military command in Paris.

He justified his decision by precedent: the files relating to Marshal Bazaine's court-martial had been treated in the same manner.[3] Memories of the crippling treason committed by a French marshal and of its dire consequences were so vivid in the minds of the top brass that they exacerbated the army's sensitivities and reactions to the apparent spying for Germany by an officer posted to the General Staff, an institution so highly prized that it was referred to as *l'Arche sainte,* the Holy Ark.

The effort to rehabilitate the French army began rapidly after the defeat. It included the reinstitution of universal military service and a determined effort to profit from the Prussian example: hence a new emphasis on intelligence work and mastery of military doctrine, exemplified by the creation of the Ecole supérieure de guerre, which admitted officers as students only on the basis of a competitive examination. The percentage of the national budget devoted to the military grew dramatically, and the army's equipment began to undergo continual modernization. The artillery received special attention since French artillery weapons, unlike the infantrymen's rifles, had been conspicuously outclassed during the war. Germany followed these developments closely. As the bordereau showed, Esterhazy had undertaken to sell Schwartzkoppen secrets relating to the 120-millimeter short cannon, knowing that they were certain to whet the attaché's appetite. That weapon was succeeded by a more powerful cannon, the 150-millimeter, and in 1897 by the "French 75," which was to play a major role in stopping the German advance in 1914. The African and Colonial Corps of the new French army had been thrown into foreign adventures: before the Dreyfus case, in Tunisia, other parts of Africa, and Indochina; in 1895 in Madagascar; and beginning in April 1900 in China, as part of the force dispatched by eight powers to suppress the Boxer Rebellion. But foreign adventures were not universally popular in France; a broad segment of the French public and politicians believed that the army's true mission was to recover France's lost provinces.

There was in addition a widely shared perception that in a country reeling from the impact of internecine political conflicts, financial and political scandals, and threatened coups, the army alone stood as an unsullied institution, the ultimate source of national stability and pride. These political conflicts included struggles that pitted republicans, who supported the Third Republic brought into being after the fall of Napoleon III, against royalists and Bonapartists, who did not accept its legitimacy; republican and anti-republican parties against socialists; and anti-clericalists against the clergy and its partisans. Attacks by revolutionary anarchists targeted political figures and the state. Eighteen eighty-two brought the collapse of Union Générale, a Catholic bank with strong ties to the church. The fall was blamed on the machinations of Jewish bankers, collectively personified by the head of the French Rothschild family, Baron Alphonse de Rothschild. A peculiarly French scandal erupted in the fall of 1887: it was discovered that generals as well as senators and other politicians were trafficking in honors and decorations, including the Legion of Honor, which had been peddled by one Daniel Wilson, the son-in-law of Charles Grévy, the president of the republic, from an office in the Elysée palace. Grévy resigned and was succeeded by Sadi Carnot, a veteran but obscure politician, who was murdered by an anarchist in June 1894. Two years earlier, in 1892, the Panama Canal Company scandal had erupted, exposing widespread corruption among the political class, as the company crashed under a mountain of debt and thousands of investors lost their savings. In addition to these conflicts, in 1877, there had been a near coup by the monarchist and archconservative Marshal Mac-Mahon, and for several years beginning in 1887 it seemed certain that Georges Boulanger, a fabulously popular general with broad appeal across the political spectrum of French society, from the royalist far right to the working class, would overthrow the republic. Boulangism, his movement, fizzled unexpectedly on April Fool's Day 1889, when the general, distracted by a love affair or suffering from a loss of nerve, fled France for Belgium instead of leading his followers, who were ready to march on the Elysée. Cutting across all other quarrels was the struggle over the role of the Catholic church in education and the state, which the church lost when a law voted in on December 9, 1905, terminated the concordat between France and the Vatican and provided for a strict separation between church and state.

Even if due allowance is made for this background, the public relations success of the reinvented army was astonishing. De Gaulle described brilliantly the enthusiasm for the army of the post–Franco-Prussian War generations, which swelled the enrollment at Saint-Cyr, the venerable French military academy, and at other newly created military academies, the admission to which was based on competitive examination. Particularly important as the source of young officers was the elite Ecole polytechnique, whose graduates, like Dreyfus, were choosing the army as a career. The French officer, de Gaulle wrote, "loves his profession, which procures for him privileges of action and authority. The pay is meager, but the officer enjoys singular social prestige. In a garrison town, everyone shows him respect. Merchants have confidence in him. He is at the center of festivities. Society appreciates his bearing. Women are well disposed toward him. Families are glad to take for a son-in-law that man of honor, of whom it is said that 'he has a future' and in any case assured wages, and later a pension."[4]

Marcel Proust, a keen observer of French society at the fin de siècle, traced the French love affair with the army in *A la recherche du temps perdu*. We see it when the townspeople of Combray, the town where the narrator's family has its roots, turn out to watch the regiment go by; in the attitude of the Duke and Duchess of Guermantes, quintessential snobs whom nothing would induce to attend a garden party or dinner at the Elysée but who invite to their exclusive dinners General de Froberville for no reason other than his military rank; in the exalted fervor of the prince de Guermantes's expression of his love for the army; and, of course, in the military career of the Guermantes' nephew, Robert de St. Loup.

At the summit of the idolized army stood a new institution, the army General Staff, organized along the lines of the Prussian General Staff, which had been generally credited with Prussia's victory in 1870. Its task was the sort of detailed planning for contingencies that had been lacking when France lurched into that war. In October 1890, the rank of chief of the General Staff was created, and General François de Miribel became the first incumbent. Son, brother, and father of *polytechniciens,* he was a reformer by temperament and conviction. One of his innovations, designed to break the hold on the General Staff of an old-boy network of aristocratic officers educated in Jesuit schools, was to provide that each year the twelve top graduates of the Ecole supérieure de guerre would serve on the staff as trainees, a position, however, that did not necessarily lead to a regular posting. This is how Captain Dreyfus, having graduated from the Ecole on November 19, 1892, in ninth place, obtained his appointment. On January 1, 1893, he reported for duty at the General Staff. Unfortunately for him, nine months later Miribel succumbed to a stroke while on maneuvers. General de Boisdeffre, Dreyfus's nemesis, became the new chief.

Was it reasonable to expect, as Dreyfus apparently did, that he would be welcomed by his fellow staff officers? The answer would have to be yes if qualifications for the assignment were the only thing taken into account. His academic record was beyond reproach, and reviews by officers under whom he had served were excellent, praising his intelligence, knowledge, energy, and zeal. As we have seen, only one fault had been found repeatedly: the flat and unpleasant timbre of his voice. It was not the voice of command. On the other hand, contrary to the stereotype that held that Jews could not be taught to ride, he was an excellent horseman. But an incident at the Ecole supérieure de guerre should have been a warning: General de Bonnefond, who had served as a member of the jury that examined Dreyfus at the completion of his studies at the Ecole, gave Dreyfus a grade of nineteen out of twenty for technical knowledge, and zero for the *cote d'amour,* his personality, declaring that he did not want Jews on the General Staff, and thus reducing Dreyfus's class ranking from third to ninth out of eighty-one. Dreyfus testified at the Rennes court-martial that after reflecting on the matter he had complained to the commandant of the school, who received him courteously and assured him that the zero would have no practical effect. His ranking was still sufficient to qualify him for the coveted staff post.

Anti-Semites like General de Bonnefond were not difficult to find among high-ranking officers. Anti-Jewish feelings, reinforced by the reluctance of traditionalists to open doors to newcomers selected through competitive examinations rather than friendship, family connections, and mentoring, pervaded the General Staff. Thus, even apart from anti-Semitism, for traditionalists the unwelcome new wave was epitomized by graduates of the Ecole polytechnique, which also admitted students exclusively on the basis of their examination scores. Usually serving in the artillery, brought up on mathematics and natural sciences, and often belonging to anti-clerical families, the new students were in stark, and for the traditionalists highly unpleasant, contrast to the bourgeois or aristocratic officers who had attended educational institutions run by Jesuits. The intruders were regarded with suspicion, as unlikely to fit in with their colleagues and contribute to the maintenance of the character of the institution. When the newcomer was also a Jew, suspicion was added to the aversion. Since anti-Semites proclaimed that Jews—especially Alsatian

Jews, with their knowledge of the German language and their German-accented French—were not really French, the next step was to insinuate that Alsatian Jewish officers could not be trusted with the General Staff's important confidential information.

Nothing in Dreyfus's memoirs of the affair or his brother Mathieu's memoir indicates that Captain Dreyfus recognized the Bonnefond incident as the warning shot it was, or that he expected difficulties, or less than fair treatment, once he had entered the Holy Ark.[5] Perhaps that was due to his aloof and introverted personality and his apparent inability to communicate his feelings. He had been posted to the General Staff through a process that was based, except for the cote d'amour, solely on an arithmetical average of numerical grades. Unlike many officers—for example, Picquart, who had enjoyed the specific backing of General de Miribel and General de Galliffet on whose staff he had served—Dreyfus had no mentor or protector in a high place. He did not come from a family imbued with army lore; he had no relatives serving as officers. Nor does he seem to have made friends among his colleagues. His mode of life was not conducive to camaraderie: married, with two children, he could be counted on, except when he was on maneuvers or traveling on General Staff business, to go home every day for lunch punctually at twelve and to go straight home after work. All the same, on some level he must have been aware of the surge in France of the new virulent form of anti-Semitism. Its fountainhead was a hugely popular tract written by Edouard Drumont, *La France juive,* which sold a hundred thousand copies when it was first published in 1886; it was reprinted more than two hundred times. This compendium of pseudoscience and anti-Jewish slogans nourished an entire literature of anti-Semitic work, as well as the segment of the press that adopted anti-Semitism as its policy. French anti-Jewish propaganda was so extreme that when the Nazi weekly *Der Stürmer* began publication in the 1920s there was little new ground left for it to plow.

Beginning in 1892, *La Libre Parole,* the journal Drumont founded after the success of *La France juive,* took specific aim at Jewish officers. The shrill campaign he launched protested against the intolerably large number of Jews serving in the army, inveighing against them as a cowardly and unpatriotic race. A young officer, Captain André Crémieu-Foa, presenting himself as the representative of three hundred fellow Jewish officers on active duty, challenged Drumont to a duel. Crémieu's second was none other than Major Esterhazy, who made a sideline of befriending, and making himself useful to, rich and fashionable Jews who could be touched for an occasional loan. The duel, fought with swords, was so violent that the attending physician stopped it after both adversaries had been wounded. It had as a direct consequence another duel, this one fought with pistols, between a Jewish officer, Captain Armand Mayer, who had been Crémieu's other second, and Marquis de Morès, Drumont's crony and a notorious duelist. Mayer was killed. He had been a fellow student of Dreyfus's at the Polytechnique and was like him an Alsatian. Whatever the extent of Dreyfus's information about these and similar manifestations of the hatred gathering around Jews, he clearly suppressed the conclusions he drew and his feelings about them, thereby acting out the role that the overwhelming majority of assimilated French Jews of comparable background had assigned to themselves: to lower their heads and persist in the belief that they were full-fledged French citizens who would be protected by the republic that had granted them equal rights of citizenship.

Dreyfus was born on October 9, 1859, in Mulhouse, a large town in the southern corner of Alsace close to the German and Swiss borders. He was the seventh living child of Raphael and Jeannette (née Libmann). Two little girls had died before he was born. Raphael's father had been a peddler; his grandfather had been a kosher butcher, which was also the trade of Jeanette's father. Raphael at first worked with his father, but by the time Alfred was born his days as a peddler were over. Succeeding as a commission merchant trading in cotton, he had become rich enough to buy industrial property in Mulhouse: he was the owner of a cotton mill and counted as a substantial industrialist. To go with his new status, he constructed on a fashionable street a new four-story home that ranked with the town's more elaborate dwellings, not skimping on furniture, wall and window hangings, and other appurtenances consistent with the standing of the new residence. It was understood that the two older sons would stay at their father's side and carry on the family business while the two younger, Mathieu and Alfred, became educated men. The Franco-Prussian War disrupted the family's plans. Alsace and northern Lorraine having been formally severed from France, the parents and five of their children became subjects of the new German Reich. Henriette, an older sister who was like a second mother to Alfred, married

Joseph Valabrègue in 1870 and moved with him to Carpentras, in southwest France, where he and his family were established.

Germany gave an option to residents of the two formerly French regions: they could choose French citizenship, if they reported a new domicile in France. Raphael split the family in two: the eldest son remained in Mulhouse to run the mill, and his mother, who was too ill to be moved, stayed with him; the others, Raphael included, claimed domicile in Carpentras with Henriette Valabrègue and her husband; in reality they settled in nearby Basel in Switzerland, from which Raphael could help with the management of the mill. Shortly afterward, Alfred and Mathieu left for Paris in order to continue their education at an elite private college. Brilliant and charming, Mathieu decided against trying to pass the baccalaureate examination, which at the time was very arduous, thereby forgoing university studies. Instead, after a year of military service, he involved himself in the family business, a pursuit he abandoned when he threw himself full time into the task of seeking Alfred's exoneration. Lacking Mathieu's personal attractiveness and his breadth of intellect but conscientious to a fault, Alfred concentrated on the dreaded examination, passed it, spent two years rather than the usual three preparing for the Ecole polytechnique, and in November 1878 was admitted as one of the youngest cadets, with the rank of 182nd out of 236. Dreyfus's class standing had improved by graduation: he ranked 128th out of 235. Having chosen to serve in the artillery, he had to pass another competitive examination to gain admission to the Ecole d'application de l'artillerie. Two years later he graduated from that school, 32nd in a class of 97. In the spring of 1885, he was promoted to the rank of first lieutenant and assigned to an artillery regiment, serving first in Le Mans, a large provincial town some 155 miles west of Paris, and then with a horse-drawn cavalry unit of the regiment based in Paris.

The young officer was strikingly rich, the family business generating sufficient income for the four Dreyfus brothers to receive yearly payments ranging from ten to twenty thousand francs; moreover, Alfred could draw on the capital of the firm for up to three hundred thousand francs. In comparison, a second lieutenant's pay was less than two thousand francs per year. Family fortunes were rare in the French army of the time; only 20 percent of officers expected to inherit as much as twenty thousand francs. Dreyfus's wealth was to increase: on the death of his father in 1893, he inherited a share of the Mulhouse cotton mill. In the meantime, he had married, on April 21, 1890, the beautiful and fiercely loyal Lucie Hadamard. The Dreyfus family welcomed the connection, and so did the Hadamards, although their social standing was significantly higher. One sign of the depth of the Hadamards' integration into French bourgeoisie was that Lucie's maternal grandfather had graduated from the Polytechnique, as had her cousins, one of whom was Paul Hadamard, who had introduced Dreyfus to the family. Lucie's father dealt in diamonds, following in the steps of his grandfather and father, who were jewelers and dealers in precious stones. The family's numerous uncles and cousins were likewise solidly established and would in time become linked by marriage to the cream of French Jewish society. Like the Dreyfus clan, Lucie's family on both sides had roots in Alsace.

An officer was required to obtain permission from his commander to become engaged. It was granted if the proposed bride appeared to be of good character, and the dowry contract showed that she would bring to the marriage financial means that were sufficient in relation to the officer's rank. Those conditions were easily met: Lucie's parents were rich. Their wealth, estimated at three million francs, was reflected in Lucie's dowry, which included, in addition to the usual trousseau of linen, lace, jewelry, and furniture, a guaranteed modest income, and 160,000 francs in cash. As for her expectations, she was in line to inherit more than 500,000 francs. All in all, by October 1894, when he was accused of treason, Alfred Dreyfus had an annual income of about 40,000 francs, the family lived in a large and beautiful apartment on avenue du Trocadéro, and their style of life, including Alfred's two saddle horses, was appropriate to their ample means. He rode every morning in the Bois de Boulogne before reporting for duty. Had anyone on the General Staff paused to reflect, and had Dreyfus not been a Jew, the notion that this very rich officer was selling military secrets to the German attaché would have surely seemed absurd. But Dreyfus was Jewish, even if thoroughly assimilated, and neither General Mercier nor General de Boisdeffre, or any of their immediate subordinates, asked himself hard questions before the accusation was made.

Paradoxically, neither Dreyfus's personal wealth nor the brilliant marriage, which the army had promptly approved, had won him favor at the General Staff—or in his previous postings. His fortune had instead worked against him, playing into one of the most invidious anti-Semitic stereotypes, that of the parvenu rich

Jewish intruder, elbowing his way into positions that of right belonged to the real French, throwing his money around, and buying advantages that truly French and virtuously poorer officers could not afford. Among the plethora of venomous gossip to which witnesses at the courts-martial testified was a dreadful anecdote about Dreyfus asking another officer whether he liked to shoot game; if he did, Dreyfus's brother would be glad to get him an invitation to one of the royal shoots, hunts organized in woods appertaining to former French royal chateaus that the brother frequented. Whether the story, disdainfully repeated, was true or false, it illustrates how some, if not many, of Dreyfus's colleagues saw him.

Indeed, measured objectively, the speed of the Dreyfus family's progress to wealth and position was dizzying: it had taken only forty years (from the death in 1819 of Alfred's kosher butcher great-grandfather, who knew no French and spoke only Yiddish and perhaps some limited Alsatian German) for Raphael Dreyfus to metamorphose from peddler to industrialist and to begin building the fortune, based on a traditional French manufacturing activity, that would enable him a mere thirty years later to congratulate himself on his son Alfred's marriage, career, and household. To the distress of long-established French bourgeoisie, this was a pattern they could discern all around them. The most spectacular example was, of course, the House of Rothschild. The patriarch of the family's French branch had arrived in France from the Frankfurt ghetto in 1811, at the age of nineteen, knowing hardly any French. Working in partnership with his brothers based in Frankfurt, London, Vienna, and Naples, he became the banker of choice of the restored French monarch, Louis XVIII, and after the revolution of July 1830 that overthrew Louis's successor, Charles X, he continued as the royal banker under King Louis-Philippe.

Baron James, as he became through the grant in 1817 of an Austrian title, financed government operations, heavy industry, coal mines, and the construction of French railroads. Except for royal palaces, his chateau at Ferrières, which he bought from Joseph Fouché—one of the arch villains of French history—and subsequently enlarged, was the largest in France and so luxurious that before he died in 1868 James was able to flatter Napoleon III by inviting him out to shoot on the grounds and later lunch at the chateau. James's successor at the head of the French bank, his eldest son, Alphonse, had installed himself in the mansion at the corner of rue Saint-Florentin and rue de Rivoli that had belonged to Talleyrand and now houses the U.S. Consulate General. He continued his father's role as the most important banker in France and financed the payment ahead of the due date of the reparations France had been obliged to pay under the Treaty of Frankfurt. Alongside Dreyfus, after he had been convicted of treason, and Joseph Reinach, a left-of-center politician who became an early Dreyfusard, Baron Alphonse was by common consent the most hated man in France: the quintessential, endlessly caricatured Jew, battening on Christians and spreading disease throughout French society. But Baron Alphonse was hardly the only hugely rich Jewish banker in France: standing a step or two behind him was a phalanx of other Jewish bankers of great wealth who bore, like the Rothschilds, non-French titles: Counts Camondo and Cahen d'Anvers, Barons Koenigswarter, Léonino, d'Almeida, and Menasce. Their names, unlike that of Rothschild, are no longer recognized by the public, with the exception of Camondo, who is now remembered through the jewel-like Musée Nissim de Camondo, located in Paris in the family mansion at the edge of the Parc Monceau. After 1870, this Jewish aristocracy was joined by such banking families as Bamberger, Stern, Deutsch, Pereire, and Bischoffsheim, as well as Joseph Reinach's uncle Baron Jacques de Reinach, who committed suicide in December 1892 after having been implicated in the bribery scandal connected with the collapse of the Panama Canal Company.

The stunning success of the relatively small community of French Jews—at the turn of the century the Jewish population was estimated at eighty-six thousand out of a total French population of 39 million—was not limited to finance. In 1895, of the 260 members of the Institut de France (the collective name of the academies—Académie française, Académie des inscriptions et belles-lettres, Académie des sciences, Académie des beaux-arts, and Académie des sciences morales et politiques—of France's most eminent writers, scholars, and artists), 7 were Jews. As we have seen, there were in the 1890s about 300 Jewish officers on active duty in the army and in 1889 5 generals. There were Jewish deputies, senators, and important civil servants, including counselors on the Conseil d'Etat, the highest administrative tribunal in France, and Jewish professors at the Sorbonne, the Collège de France, the Ecole polytechnique, the Ecole normale supérieure, and the prestigious Ecole pratique des hautes études.[6]

French Jews were also represented in great numbers in medicine and the law, and in journalism, literature, the theater, and the arts. The careers the of three Reinach brothers, sometimes called the Brothers Know-It-All (*les frères je-sais-tout*), in many ways exemplified this flowering. The youngest, Théodore (1868–1928), received the greatest number of prizes of anyone in his generation at the *concours général*, a national examination administered at the end of the last year of the lycée in order to identify the best students. Having obtained doctorates in the law and in literature, he practiced for several years as a barrister (*avocat*) in Paris and then became an archeologist with a particular interest in numismatics, which he taught at the Sorbonne and the Collège de France; he also taught history of religions at the Ecole pratique des hautes études. Salomon (1858–1932) received, like Théodore, a gold medal at the concours général and became a philosopher and archeologist, directing major digs in Asia Minor, the Greek islands, and Odessa. Joseph (1856–1921), having triumphed at the concours général, also first became a lawyer. His brilliance was noticed by the great republican politician Léon Gambetta, who asked him to become his chief of staff. After Gambetta's death, Joseph became a republican politician and journalist, was twice a deputy, and became one of the first important Dreyfusards who was not a member of Dreyfus's family. He was also the author of the six-volume, monumental *Histoire de l'Affaire Dreyfus*.[7]

Putting aside such factors as the talent and will to succeed of individual Jews, the millennial Jewish tradition of literacy, and the high value Jews set on learning, the obvious reason for the scope and rapidity of their progress in French society was their early emancipation. On August 26, 1789, the constitutional assembly of "representatives of the French people" had adopted a Declaration of the Rights of Man and of the Citizen, Article 1 of which declared: "All men are born free and equal in their rights. Social distinctions may be founded only on the common good." That shining promise was fulfilled for Jews living in France when the successor revolutionary legislative body adopted the decree of September 27, 1791 (confirmed on November 13), that granted rights of citizenship with all the advantages conferred by the Constitution to "all men who take the oath of citizenship, and undertake to fulfill all the duties imposed by the Constitution." French Jews greeted the news with jubilation and flocked to mass oath-swearing ceremonies. For the first time since the Babylonian captivity they were truly free.

The significance of the promise's having been carried to its logical conclusion—no less of a logician than Robespierre was one of the proponents of citizenship for French Jews—can be best appreciated in the context of the Jews' situation at the time in Spain, the Habsburg lands, the German states, and England. The Inquisition was still persecuting Marranos, descendants of converted Jews who secretly adhered to the Jewish religion or practices. Jews in the Austrian Empire had none of the rights of citizens: unless they lived in the countryside they were confined in ghettoes; they were subject to special taxes for the privilege of living in specified areas, such as Bohemia; marriage was forbidden except by permission of the imperial administration and was usually granted only to the eldest son; and in addition to petty and vexatious restrictions on the occupations they could pursue,

Jews were precluded from owning or leasing land. The wave of revolutions, sometimes referred to as the Spring of Nations, that swept over Europe in 1848 resulted in Austria's adopting a constitution that granted freedom of religion to all minorities in the Habsburg lands and lifted the special restrictions on Jews, but a counterrevolution followed, which took away the new rights, and it was not until 1867, the year of the compromise that resulted in the foundation of the Austro-Hungarian Empire, that a new constitution granted Jews full legal rights. Although Jews did serve in the military reserves as staff and regimental officers, the number of Jewish career officers was small. Their chances of promotion were strongly dependent on whether they had converted, which was not the case in the French army.[8] Emperor Franz Joseph's Jews were also barred by custom from the civil service (except at the lowest level) and university teaching posts. In Germany, Jews served as officers in the reserves, but at the turn of the nineteenth century there were no German-Jewish career officers.

The situation varied in the German states. In certain of them, Jewish emancipation came in the wake of Napoleon's victories, but rights were withdrawn and the old restrictions returned following his defeat at Waterloo. German Jews did not become full citizens until 1871, at the unification of Germany. In England, where anti-Semitism was rife, progress was made beginning in the early years of the nineteenth century. The first Jew was admitted to the bar in 1833, and the first Jewish sheriff was appointed in 1835. Full emancipation came in 1858, and with it a change in the form of oath required of members of the House of

Commons that had the intended effect of permitting Baron Lionel de Rothschild to take his seat as a member for the City of London. Previously, his seat had been left open, although successive elections kept on returning him as a member.

The emancipation of French Jews in 1791 provoked a fierce anti-Semitic response, especially in Alsace, and the violence continued into the 1830s, with anti-Jewish riots, killings, and arson. Neither the agitation nor the outrages committed against persons and property succeeded in diminishing the Jews' enthusiasm for assuming the duties and privileges of French citizenship. Instead, they transformed their sense of gratitude for their citizenship into an unswerving patriotism and self-identification with France. They made the desirability—if not necessity—of assimilation the foundation of their modern Judaism.

Indeed, assimilation appeared to them to be the necessary corollary of emancipation, and it implied more than the acquisition of French culture.[9] Its larger meaning was social fusion, an ambition that included the reform of Jewish religion to bring it into the orbit of French modernity. The fact that the French state had been providing financial support for rabbis and synagogues since 1831 was important in this regard: rabbis understood that in addition to their religious status they had the status of French civil servants. The consequence was their loyalty to the state and respect for its interests in the manner in which they carried out their ministry. Some thinkers accepted the inevitable end result: extinguishment of Jewish feeling and the absorption of Jews into the mass of their fellow citizens of other faiths not by conversion or intermarriage but by making their daily life part of the tissue of French culture and daily activities. More frequently Jews thought that they could retain a Jewish identity and at the same time maintain and exercise their rights as full French citizens. They preferred republican France, under which they had been emancipated, but had given freely their allegiance to both the First and the Second Empire, to the restored Bourbons, and to the Orléans monarchy. As anti-Semitism grew more vehement in the 1880s, the attraction for Jews of the political center became necessarily greater. It appeared to offer more safety than the right, which represented forces of monarchism and the Catholic Church, or the left, with its anti-clerical emphasis that also threatened the continued state financial support to synagogues and rabbis and its anti-bourgeois bias.

The desire to be above all else and at all times French had another consequence: the tendency of French Jews to minimize the importance of anti-Semitism, remain passive, and avoid speaking out against outrageous behavior, a tendency that was replicated in Germany during the years immediately preceding Hitler's coming to power and afterward, during the short period when he was still vulnerable to international pressure. In his memoir of the affair Léon Blum wrote that at first,

> as a general matter, Jews had accepted the conviction of Dreyfus as definitive and just. They did not speak of the case among themselves; far from raising it, they fled from the subject. A great sorrow had fallen upon Israel. One suffered it without saying a word, waiting for time and silence to erase its effects.
>
> Jews as a whole even greeted with a good deal of circumspection and distrust the beginnings of the campaign for judicial review. The dominant feeling expressed itself by a formula such as this: "This is

not something with which Jews should get mixed up . . ." Not all elements in that complex sentiment were of equal quality. There was, certainly, patriotism and even irritable patriotism, respect for the army, confidence in its chiefs, and repugnance for considering them biased or fallible. But there was also a sort of selfish and fearful prudence that could be characterized in more severe terms. Jews did not want it to be believed that they defended Dreyfus because he was a Jew.[10]

Jewish attempts to be discreet proved as unavailing in 1894 in France as they would in the 1930s in Germany. As soon as it became known that Dreyfus had been arrested and charged with treason, anti-Semitic newspapers launched a campaign focused on him but at the same time claiming that the entire Jewish community was united to defend the traitor and carry forward his work of espionage. The term *Syndicat* (Syndicate) came into use, invented and propagated by Drumont, the author of *La France juive,* and Henri de Rochefort, a right-wing journalist: it was intended to denote an alliance of Jews drawing on the vast reservoir of Jewish money and determined to use every corrupt means to defend Dreyfus. Anyone coming to the defense of Dreyfus risked being accused of being a member of this Syndicate or in its pay. Once it became known that Lieutenant Colonel Picquart was determined to prove that Dreyfus was innocent and Esterhazy the traitor, the anti-Dreyfusard press began to refer to Picquart regularly as the principal agent of the Syndicate.

The Dreyfus family was acutely conscious of the danger of giving substance to the conspiracy theory. In the beginning Mathieu did everything he could to avoid publicity, although it finally seemed possible for him to engage Bernard Lazare to prepare an exposé demonstrating the judicial error committed by the 1894 court-martial and distribute it widely, and for Lucie Dreyfus to petition the Chamber of Deputies for a judicial review. It was a choice that in the view of some Dreyfusards delayed significantly the ultimate success of the protest. But it proved prescient when the wave of attacks on Jews commenced after the Dreyfus Affair had gone public and Zola had published his "J'accuse." As Michael R. Marrus has written:

> Immediately following the publication of Émile Zola's *J'accuse,* there were anti-Jewish uprisings in virtually every city in France. Not only were Jewish stores and places attacked and burned but Jews were assaulted in the streets. The police seemed to be either ineffective or in league with the rioters. . . . According to police reports the crowds were not only crying slogans related to the Dreyfus Affair, but also "Death to the Jews!" In Paris the mob burst out of its traditional battle ground in the Latin Quarter to attack Jewish stores on the Right Bank. In Nantes, it was reported, a number of soldiers joined in the demonstration, and in Bordeaux pitched battles were fought in the vicinity of the synagogue. Significant outbreaks were reported in Marseille, Lyon, Nancy, and Versailles. Even smaller towns, Clermont-Ferrand, La Rochelle, Poitiers, Angoulême, and Saint-Flour[,] had incidents of violence and anti-Semitic demonstrations. In Algeria, where for several days the police did nothing to prevent the clashes, the riots were particularly bloody; several people were beaten to death in what could only be described as a pogrom.[11]

Stoking the fires of anti-Semitism were reactionary Catholic publications, among them *La Croix,* a newspaper with a large circulation, which called for the expulsion of Jews from France.

Eighteen ninety-nine was a year of extreme political tension in France, much of it related to the progress through the Court of

Cassation of the review of Dreyfus's court-martial. Under the legislation then applicable, once the petition for review was accepted, the task of examining the Paris court-martial's judgment belonged to the criminal chamber of the Court of Cassation. Charges of bias in favor of Dreyfus on the part of the judges of that chamber resulted in new legislation that transferred jurisdiction from the criminal chamber to a united chamber composed of all the judges of both the criminal chamber and the civil chambers. While the united chamber laboriously reviewed the findings of the criminal chamber judges, who in accordance with the old law had been charged with reporting on the case, Paul Déroulède, a former follower of General Boulanger and the founder of the right-wing Ligue des Patriotes, attempted a coup d'état on the day of the state funeral of the president of the republic, Félix Faure. The coup fizzled. Déroulède was at first acquitted by Court of Assizes in Paris and then banished for five years by a vote of the Senate. After the Court of Cassation reversed the 1894 judgment on June 3 and remanded Dreyfus to a court-martial in Rennes, the news was greeted by a storm of nationalist and anti-Semitic agitation. Much of the rage was directed at Emile Loubet, Faure's successor. He was suspected of being a Dreyfusard and, for good measure, of having been complicit in the Panama Company scandal. On June 4, Loubet was set upon at the racetrack in Auteuil by a monarchist baron, who hit him on the head with a cane. Fortunately, the president was wearing a top hat, and no harm was done. A huge counter-demonstration by republicans and Dreyfusards took place in Paris, followed by violence in the streets. For the first time, the army gave signs of restiveness: generals in Rennes and Angers issued inflammatory orders of the day, protesting the review of Dreyfus's conviction, and signed letters that were published in the anti-Semitic press. Later that summer the government fell, and after a false start a new government charged with the defense of the republic was formed with Pierre Waldeck-Rousseau as prime minister and General de Galliffet as minister of war, infuriating the anti-Semitic and anti-Dreyfusard press and adherents, who widely believed that Waldeck-Rousseau was a Dreyfusard. Galliffet was attacked as an ally of Joseph Reinach and the butcher of the Paris Commune.

The court-martial in Rennes began on August 7 and ended on September 9 with the verdict of guilty against Dreyfus. Throughout that period, Rennes resembled an armed camp, with a huge concentration of police and military to contain the anti-Dreyfusard agitation. Even so, on August 14, Ferdinand Labori, Zola's counsel, who had joined Edgar Demange as a member of the defense team, was shot at and wounded by an assailant, who escaped and was never apprehended. The presidential pardon for Dreyfus was signed on September 19, but it was not publicly announced until the evening in order to make it possible for Dreyfus to leave the military prison before the anti-Dreyfusard mob exploded. The chief of the Sûreté, the controller general of the Ministry of the Interior, and three detectives accompanied Dreyfus from the prison to the train station, then took the train with him to Nantes, where Mathieu was waiting for him. From there the party traveled to Bordeaux, changed trains for Avignon, and finished the journey by carriage to the property of the Dreyfuses' sister in Carpentras. The tension was so great that the chief of the Sûreté had made certain that Mathieu was armed.

Violence and threats of violence would continue to track Dreyfus. Zola died September 29, 1902, asphyxiated in his bed by carbon monoxide fumes from the bedroom stove; the chimney was found to have blocked, giving rise to the suspicion that it had been tampered with by extreme rightists who had been calling for his assassination. The question of responsibility, or indeed of whether there had been foul play, has never been resolved. Zola's widow asked Dreyfus to stay away from the funeral at the cemetery in Montmartre, which was to be held a week later. She was concerned that his presence would set off demonstrations and put him and other mourners in danger. The prefect of police agreed, but Dreyfus, who had become very close to Zola, refused to follow the advice. A riot ensued at the cemetery, stimulated by the anti-Semitic press, and it took a charge by mounted troops to disperse the mob. In the meantime, Dreyfus, who had been surrounded by Mathieu and friends forming a human shield, escaped by a side gate. That experience, and the need for police protection when he went to his father-in-law's funeral two weeks later, convinced Dreyfus that he must abstain from attending public events, a decision that kept him from attending the funeral of his brother-in-law, the husband of his beloved sister Henriette, and, less than a year later, that of Bernard Lazare, whose brochure had been essential in launching the public campaign for judicial review. Dreyfus's absence from the latter was criticized by the press, and the bitterness against Dreyfus was great. In his memoir of the period, first published in

1910, Lazare's friend, the great poet Charles Péguy, reproached Dreyfus and his family for having considered Lazare a hired hand, someone who could be treated with contempt.[12]

Six years later the government approved the transfer of Zola's remains to the Panthéon, an honor reserved for France's heroes. Right-wing extremists, monarchists, and anti-Semites, allied with Action française, a new right-wing royalist group, exploded with fury, expressed in scabrous articles that appeared in the organization's newly created newspaper. An undercover police agent reported that a royalist had put a twenty-thousand-franc bounty on Dreyfus's head. The ceremony at the Panthéon took place in the midst of hostile demonstrations. Although violence had been foreseen, Dreyfus attended with his wife and children and was fired upon by an extremist right-wing journalist, Louis-Anthelme Gregori. Warned by the first shot, which miscarried, and seeing the weapon aimed at him, Dreyfus raised his right arm to protect himself. The arm was pierced, but it had deflected the bullet and saved him from greater harm. Gregori was acquitted on the ground that the attack, prompted by passion, had not been premeditated. Léon Daudet, son of the famous writer Alphonse Daudet and an anti-Semite and royalist associated with Action française who had actively instigated the anti-Zola and anti-Dreyfusard agitation around the ceremony, referred to the incident in his memoir of the period as a "joke of an attack by our old colleague Gregori, of the *Gaulois* [an anti-Semitic right-wing newspaper], against the famous Dreyfus, twice convicted, then pardoned, then absolved by a sleight of hand."[13]

The excesses—in rhetoric and in action—of anti-Semites and

far-right-wing movements (monarchist, clericalist, and extreme nationalist) strengthened the resolve of those in France who wanted to buttress its republican institutions. The Radical Party, a left-of-center parliamentary group, won in the 1902 elections and became the mainstay of the Third Republic. It was anti-clerical and opposed to colonial expansion, forced the retirement of anti-republican generals, and brought the army under firm civilian control. Nevertheless, anti-republicanism and anti-Semitism continued to be potent forces in France through the 1930s and into the Vichy years.

Dreyfus died on July 12, 1935, his health having worsened over his last few years. He had lived long enough to read about, if not to see, the violent demonstrations on February 6, 1934, staged by armed anti-republican, clericalist, and anti-Semitic leagues. Had he lived a few years longer, he would have witnessed the rise of the Front populaire, a coalition of left-wing groups, including the Communist Party, brought into being the following year in reaction to those riots and the perceived danger of a proto-fascist coup. The Front populaire won the legislative elections in May 1936 and formed a cabinet with the early Dreyfusard Léon Blum as prime minister. The presence of a Jew at the head of the government enraged anti-Semites, who called openly for his assassination. The Front populaire remained in office only two years, its tenure marked by violent strikes involving confrontations between the strikers and police, rioting by adherents of Action française and the even more extreme and fascistic Cagoule, a failed attempt to assassinate Blum, a bomb attack in September 1936 against the Cagoule's head office in Paris that the Cagoule had staged with the intention of blaming it on Communists, and the coup attempted by the Cagoule in November of that year. The anti-republicans' yearning for an authoritarian regime found full expression in Marshal Pétain's Vichy. Its anti-Semitic policies that were harsher even than the Nuremburg laws in their definition of a Jew, and its eagerness to cooperate with Germany in the deportation of French Jews to German concentration camps, have become well known since the publication in 1972 of Robert O. Paxton's groundbreaking *Vichy France: Old Guard and New Order, 1940–1944*. Vichy authorities in fact turned Blum over to the Germans, but he survived his deportation to Buchenwald, where he was treated with circumspection, and until his death in 1950 he played an important role in the reconstruction of France.

Racism and anti-republicanism have continued to haunt France since World War II. They were on display in the torture of Algerians during the war for independence that raged in Algeria from 1954 until March 1962, when it ended with the signature of the Evian Agreements; in General de Gaulle's coup d'état in May 1958; in the putsch of French generals in Algeria in April 1961; and in the attempt to assassinate de Gaulle and his wife in Petit Clamart on August 22, 1962, to name only a few incidents. On October 3, 1980, a bomb exploded in front of the synagogue on rue Copernic, in the sixteenth arrondissement of Paris; four persons were killed and some twenty wounded. If the explosion had taken place a few minutes later, the number of victims would have been far greater because the Sabbath service would have ended and the faithful would have been leaving the synagogue. The attack was the occasion of an unforgettable comment by the French prime minister of the time, Raymond Barre, who referred to the "innocent French victims" of the crime. Initially, it was thought that the attack was the work of the French extreme right. More than twenty years later, the presumed terrorist was found: a Lebanese of Palestinian descent who had since acquired Canadian nationality and was living peacefully in Canada after a long sojourn in the United States.

A pattern of outrages against Jews has held steady: numerous instances of desecration of Jewish cemeteries and arson of synagogues are but one example. In recent years, racism and religious hatred have afflicted disfavored suburbs of Paris and other French cities, often erupting in violence committed by black Africans and Muslims against a society they view as hostile and fundamentally unfair, and against Jews, whom they hate for being Jews and because they hate Israel. Anti-Semitic attacks have included in the last several years cases of kidnapping and torture, the most notorious of which was the kidnapping for ransom of Ilan Halimi, a young Jewish cellphone salesman, by a gang of French-educated youths, some of whom were Muslim immigrants and some white and of French descent. Halimi endured three weeks of torture that included beatings, burns, cuts on the face and the body, and threats of sodomization with a broomstick. At the end, acid was poured over his body, his throat was cut, and his body was drenched with gasoline and set on fire. The chief of the gang of kidnappers denied that anti-Semitism had been a motive: Halimi had been kidnapped because Jews have money.

3

"what do you care if that jew stays on devil's island?"

In his memoir of the affair, Mathieu Dreyfus recalled the months that followed the degradation ceremony at the Ecole militaire: "There was a void around us. The fevered agitation of the struggle, when we alternated between hope and despair, had disappeared. Silence, a silence of death, hung over us. It seemed to us that we were no longer human beings like the others, that we had been cut off from the world of the living, struck to the heart by a mortal illness. A few intimates, out of compassion, continued to bring . . . words of consolation. They gave me the impression of people who thought the struggle was impossible, that the affair had ended."[1] Indeed, the situation must have seemed hopeless. Dreyfus's appeal to a military review commission had been summarily denied. That made the court-martial's judgment final, with no further right of review. Dreyfus stood convicted of treason. The fact that seven military judges—officers in the revered French army—had reached the verdict unanimously had had enormous influence on public opinion, precluding any doubt about Dreyfus's guilt. French Jews felt that he had disgraced himself, his family, and the entire Jewish community. Léon Blum recalled that Jews of Dreyfus's age and social class who had also reached high positions in the army or civil service having scored well on tough competitive examinations, took his crime personally: they resented the thought that anti-Semites would use it against them, putting in doubt their probity and patriotism, and endangering their exemplary careers. They wanted Dreyfus and his case to be forgotten.

In these circumstances, Mathieu Dreyfus decided that the first step must be to attempt to convince family friends, and as broad a circle of acquaintances as possible, that in spite of all appearances his brother was innocent. At a minimum he hoped to shake their belief in Alfred's guilt. He urged those whom he managed to convince to seek recruits for the cause. As these efforts gradually met with success and became known, they lent grist to the mill of anti-Semitic journalists and anyone else who wanted to believe in the myth of a Jewish Syndicate, a conspiracy with unlimited access to gold and power, that was doing battle on Dreyfus's behalf. In reality, the early Dreyfusards were neither rich nor powerful, but three of them, Major Ferdinand Forzinetti, Bernard Lazare, and Dr. Joseph Gibert, gave assistance that proved crucially important.

Forzinetti was the commander of the rue du Cherche-midi military prison, where Dreyfus had been held since his arrest. Dreyfus's passionate and unwavering protestations of innocence, and his general demeanor—which in Forzinetti's long experience with prisoners were all inconsistent with guilt—had convinced him that Dreyfus was innocent. He never wavered in that belief. Forzinetti's espousal of Dreyfus's cause and advocacy on his behalf eventually led to his exclusion from the army. A few days after Dreyfus's transfer from the Cherche-midi prison to the prison on the Ile de Ré, en route to Devil's Island, Forzinetti gave Mathieu the prosecution's act of indictment with Alfred's notes in the margins; it would later serve as a roadmap for his defenders. Even more valuable was an introduction: Forzinetti put Mathieu in contact with Bernard Lazare, a gifted young literary critic who was rapidly establishing his reputation for astuteness, tough argumentation, and independence. Having previously convinced Lazare of Dreyfus's innocence and taken the measure of his enthusiasm, Forzinetti told Mathieu that he thought this was someone who could find allies in literary and journalistic circles. Mathieu followed Forzinetti's advice and asked Lazare to undertake that task; Lazare's effectiveness may be judged by Léon Blum's conversion to the cause. Blum recalled that an older friend, Michel Bréal, the "father of semantics," told him that he did not believe in Dreyfus's guilt because no intelligible motive for the crime had been advanced. Blum became a convinced Dreyfusard somewhat later, after a visit from Lazare, who had brought Forzinetti with him. Lazare proved irresistible. "With admirable self-abnegation, indifferent to rebuffs and even suspicions," Blum wrote, Lazare "looked for support everywhere, he carried from door to door the testimony of Forzinetti and the report of counter experts [on handwriting]."[2] Dr. Gibert, a Le Havre physician, had also been troubled by the lack of motive for the alleged crime and, like Forzinetti, by Dreyfus's unwavering insistence that he had been falsely accused; as a physician he feared that the climate of Devil's Island would kill the prisoner, a concern that added an element of urgency to his advocacy.

Mathieu could take satisfaction and comfort from seeing that the circle of men and women who did not accept the guilty verdict and sought ways to overturn it was growing. In other respects, Mathieu's efforts in 1895 failed. Agents of the Sûreté and the Statistics Section harassed him and his family by clumsy surveillance and attempts to ferret out information by bribing his domestic staff; he was obliged to rent apartments and houses under assumed names, and to send his children away to stay with his wife's parents for their protection. The harassment and the dirty tricks would continue for the next four years. Two fortuitous developments in the first part of the year, however, opened the way to ultimate success. Toward the end of February, Dr. Gibert reported to Mathieu a conversation in which no less a personage than Félix Faure, the president of the republic, had told him that Dreyfus had not been convicted on the basis of the bordereau or anything that transpired at the hearings. Instead, the judges had reached the guilty verdict after reading documents given to them in secret while they were deliberating. For reasons of state, it had been impossible to show these documents to the accused or his counsel. Faure had rejected Gibert's entreaties that he intervene on behalf of Dreyfus, but surprisingly he authorized the doctor to tell Mathieu about the secret documents. Mathieu recognized at once the extraordinary potential significance of this information as the basis of a judicial challenge to the legality of the military tribunal's proceedings. Soon afterward the accuracy of President Faure's disclosures was reinforced: Demange, Dreyfus's lawyer, trying to track down a rumor circulating among his colleagues that the military judges had seen a letter from one foreign military attaché in Paris to another in which reference was made to "cette canaille de D.," asked his friend Ludovic Trarieux whether the story had any substance.

Trarieux had become minister of justice in January 1895, when a short-lived government led by Alexandre Ribot replaced the Dupuy government in which General Mercier had been minister of war. Trarieux confirmed the existence of the letter, giving as his source a cabinet colleague, Gabriel Hanotaux, who had remained foreign minister in the new government. (As we have seen, Hanotaux had objected to the court-martial of Dreyfus because he foresaw problems arising with Germany if the German military attaché were exposed as a spy.) However, when Demange asked Trarieux whether the other part of the story—that the letter had been given to the military judges in secret while they were deliberating—was equally true, Trarieux exclaimed that such an act could not have taken place because it would have constituted a monstrous violation of Dreyfus's rights. Trarieux subsequently became a confirmed Dreyfusard, and after he left office in November 1895 he founded the French League for the Defense of Human Rights, which made the Dreyfus case its first cause. Somewhat later in 1895, Mathieu made a remarkably astute decision. He expanded Lazare's mission by giving him all the information about the case he had collected, including everything that he had learned from Dr. Gibert and Demange, and asked Lazare to write a pamphlet demonstrating that Dreyfus was the victim of a judicial error. Lazare agreed and, disregarding the risks to which he would be exposed, told Mathieu that he would sign the pamphlet with his own name.

Up to the fall of 1896 Mathieu's other efforts were largely unsuccessful; in fact, one of his plans misfired. An English journalist, whom he had charged with keeping the Dreyfus case alive in the press by stimulating news articles about him, on his own initiative planted a story that appeared in an English newspaper on September 3 announcing that Dreyfus had escaped from Devil's Island. As we have seen, the government's frenetic response to this fabrication resulted in punitive measures against Dreyfus, allegedly taken in order to prevent a real escape. However, the appearance soon afterward of several further newspaper articles led to a breakthrough. A travel report published in *Le Figaro* on September 8 revealed the inhuman conditions of Dreyfus's incarceration and for the first time aroused stirrings of sympathy for the prisoner outside the Dreyfusard circle. A week later Demange's friend Paul de Cassagnac, a Bonapartist politician and journalist who was famous for the number of duels he had fought, discussed the possibility that Dreyfus was innocent in an article entitled "Le Doute" (The Doubt) that appeared in *L'Autorité,* a political journal of moderate conservative views. Then, on September 9 and 15, two articles in *L'Eclair,* a right-wing anti-Semitic newspaper hostile to Dreyfus, revealed in startling detail the existence of the dossier secret and its contents. The articles' intended purpose was to urge the government to publish the secret documents that had led the military judges to convict Dreyfus and thus put an end to questions about his guilt as well as to expressions of pity for him. The unintended result was to make known for the first time the extent of criminal misconduct at the court-martial.

The government did not respond to the *Eclair* articles, and that crucial silence gave Mathieu the opening he had been waiting for: until then, fearful that the government would deny the existence of the dossier, he had not dared make public use of the information he had obtained from Dr. Gibert and, through Demange, from Trarieux, or to use it as the basis of a petition for judicial review. With that obstacle removed, on September 18 Lucie Dreyfus sent a letter to the Chamber of Deputies. The undisclosed delivery to the military judges of the dossier secret, she wrote, was "a denial of justice," a violation of the fundamental rights of the defendant, and an urgent reason for overturning the court-martial's judgment.[3] The text of Lucie's letter appeared in *Le Figaro* and a number of other newspapers. The chamber rejected the petition in November, but not before Lazare's brochure, which had been ready for some time, was distributed on November 7 and 8 to all deputies and senators, as well as to leading journalists, scholars, and literary figures.[4] Completing the cycle of unexpected newspaper revelations, another right-wing newspaper, *Le Matin,* published on November 10 a facsimile of the bordereau. Its appearance in print provoked a storm within the Statistics Section and a fruitless search for the culprit who had leaked it. Much later it was discovered that *Le Matin*'s source was Pierre Teyssonières, one of the handwriting experts retained in 1894 by the Section. He confessed that he had retained the copy given to him to analyze and sold it to the newspaper. Notwithstanding efforts he had been making since the court-martial, Mathieu had been unable to obtain a facsimile of that crucial document. Seeing the bordereau for the first time and being able to examine it enabled Mathieu to assert authoritatively, with the support of the numerous distinguished experts he retained, that the handwriting was not his brother's. He was also able to commence the search for the real traitor.

The chamber's refusal to take favorable action on Lucie Dreyfus's petition was no surprise, but it had the effect of stopping the effort to free Dreyfus dead in its tracks. Under French legislation the only remaining judicial remedy was review by the Court of Cassation. While the military justice system was usually outside the Court's purview, court-martial judgments were subject to review by it if significant new facts could be adduced that had not been known at the time of the court-martial and were, on their face, of sufficient importance to warrant modification or reversal. The catch was that review was not available to petitioners as a matter of right. Only the government could request review of a court-martial judgment. If such a request were made, and after preliminary review entrusted to a group of judges it was deemed well founded, the appeal would be heard. Since the government in power at the time, led by Prime Minister Jules Méline, was opposed to reopening Dreyfus's case, any subsequent petition addressed to it was unlikely to fare any better. The difficulty of securing government action was illustrated by later developments. After the legislative elections in May 1898, the Méline government resigned and was succeeded on June 28 by a new government headed by Henri Brisson, who was more open to judicial review than Méline. Nevertheless, the new government did not authorize the minister of justice to request review by the Court until September, and then only because it had been forced to do so by a series of extraordinary developments that made such action politically imperative.

Those developments had as their root cause a personnel change at the army General Staff that occurred on July 1, 1895. Mathieu was probably unaware of it; it is doubtful whether he would have been able to appreciate its significance. On that date, Major Georges Picquart, the officer who had greeted Dreyfus at the door of the Ministry of War on the morning of his arrest and had been General Mercier's emissary at the court-martial, became the new chief of the Statistics Section, taking the place of Lieutenant Colonel Sandherr, who was suffering from last stage of general paralysis.

Born in Strasbourg in 1854, Picquart was descended from an established Catholic family of magistrates, civil servants, and soldiers. His grandfather had been the director of military warehouses in Strasbourg; his father was the Strasbourg inspector of direct taxes. Deeply marked by the French defeat in the war of 1870 and the annexation by Germany of French provinces—as had been Dreyfus, five years his junior—and for that reason, like Dreyfus, very patriotic, Picquart decided to make his career in the army. That decision as well was mirrored by Dreyfus's, but, unlike Dreyfus, Picquart did not attend the Ecole polytechnique. Instead, he went to Saint-Cyr, the oldest and most traditional of the French military academies, graduating fifth in his class. Training at the army college that was the predecessor of the Ecole supérieure de guerre and service in Algeria followed. In 1883 he was posted for the first time to the Ministry of War; in 1885, he fought in Indochina with sufficient valor and distinction to be awarded the Croix de Guerre. Upon his return to France in 1888, he was promoted to the rank of major at the unusually young age of thirty-three. Two years later he became a professor at the Ecole supérieure de guerre, and he was still teaching there, as well as serving on General de Galliffet's staff, in 1893, when General de Miribel, at the time the chief of the army General Staff, arranged for his transfer to that Holy Ark of the French army. It would have been difficult, perhaps impossible, to arrive at the General Staff with higher qualifications or more powerful backing. According to his biographer Francis de Pressensé, Picquart's general culture was on a par with his military attainments; he was fluent in German, English, Spanish, and Italian and had found a way to reconcile his teaching duties at the Ecole supérieure de guerre with the study of Russian at the celebrated Ecole des langues orientales in Paris.[5] Unmarried and fond of society and music, this paragon also found time to visit his widowed mother in Versailles almost daily and to conduct a passionate but discreet affair with the wife of a French foreign service officer. Paléologue recalled Picquart as "tall, slim, elegant, with a fine mind, both judicious and caustic, usually concealed behind an air of distant and stuffy reserve."[6] It was this model officer, incarnating all the traditions of the army and the army General Staff—including a dose of conventional anti-Semitism—who became Dreyfus's champion and savior.[7] The coincidence of his having had Dreyfus as one of his students at the Ecole supérieure de guerre had not been a factor in his advocacy: the relations between the two officers had been no more than correct. Moreover, until he had made the discoveries that obliged him to change his mind, Picquart had believed that Dreyfus was guilty. The simple and monolithic reason for Picquart's actions was his rectitude.

We have seen the conspiratorial measures taken by General Mercier and his subordinates at the General Staff in January 1895, as the general was leaving office, to cover his tracks: the destruction of du Paty's memorandum, the dispersal of the documents, and the oath he required Boisdeffre, Gonse, Sandherr, du Paty, and Henry to take never to reveal anything related to the court-martial. Those tasks having been accomplished, the Dreyfus case did not trouble the repose of the Statistics Section for the balance of that year or the first two months of 1896. The calm ended in the first part of March for a reason no one would have anticipated: Schwartzkoppen had lost patience with Esterhazy. He was dissatisfied with the information he was receiving, and during Esterhazy's visit to the German embassy on February 20 he threatened him with the termination of their relationship. In his notebooks Schwartzkoppen does not mention whether Esterhazy promised to provide better service in the future, but if such promises were made, they did not appease the military attaché. In the first part of March, Schwartzkoppen sent to Esterhazy the missive that came to be known as the *petit bleu,* the name commonly given to letters written on a special blue paper that were pneumatically propelled within Paris from post office to post office through a system of pipes. Such a letter could reach an addressee in Paris within hours. The envelope showed Esterhazy's name, rank, and home address. The letter was written in French in the sort of bureaucratic style that a German intelligence officer could be expected to use in correspondence with his agent:

> Dear Sir,
>
> I await a more detailed explanation than that which you gave me the other day on the question that was left open. In consequence, I ask that you give it to me in writing so that I may be able to judge whether I can continue my relations with the house of R.
>
> C. t.[8]

According to Marcel Thomas, the author of the most penetrating study of the malefactions of the General Staff cabal, this document—the first in the course of the affair in which the name Esterhazy appeared—arrived torn in pieces at the Statistics Section through the voie normale: the cleaning woman, Madame Bastian. Thomas believes that it was a draft that had been discarded and thrown into the wastebasket, which would explain why the envelope had not been stamped by the post office. His theory is the only one that explains satisfactorily why it had been possible for the petit bleu to come into the Section's possession:

had it been posted, it would have been received by Esterhazy. His mail was not being seized or opened by the post office, so there was no reason why it would have been intercepted. Once Esterhazy had read it, he and not Schwartzkoppen would have thrown it out—for instance, into his own wastebasket or the gutter. In such a case it would never have been picked up or stolen by an agent of the Statistics Section and quite possibly Esterhazy would never have been identified as the author of the bordereau. Thomas explains the fact that the handwriting on the petit bleu was not Schwartzkoppen's by his having preferred to dictate it to a secretary or a junior embassy employee. The signature, however, was one that Schwartzkoppen regularly used.[9]

Schwartzkoppen's recollection of the petit bleu was different. He claimed that he had written the petit bleu, and recalled depositing it personally in the mailbox.[10] He speculated that one of the Statistics Section agents who had been tailing him must have retrieved it. Thomas's version seems more credible, although it contradicts directly Schwartzkoppen's statement that he had written the letter. As we have seen, Schwartzkoppen also claimed not to have thrown the bordereau into his wastebasket. He may have wished to obscure in his memoir the embarrassing habitual carelessness with which he handled sensitive documents. Moreover, there was no reason for anyone at the Section to have invented the story of Madame Bastian's having delivered a torn petit bleu.

In accordance with a new procedure instituted by Picquart, documents received through the usual channel were brought first to him. Henry being away on leave, he instructed Captain Lauth to piece the bits of blue paper back together. Once that was done they both realized its great importance: they held in their hands evidence that the German military attaché, known to the Statistics Section for his intelligence activities, was writing to a French army major in terms that could not have been more suspicious. And here began a series of missteps that would later create a serious problem for Picquart. He asked Lauth to photograph the reconstituted document, telling him that he intended to make it appear as though the petit bleu had been seized by the post office. This might have made sense if the purpose had been to use this incriminating document outside the Statistics Section without revealing the activities of Madame Bastian. But the sender's name did not appear on the envelope. Thus, if it were made to appear that the petit bleu had been seized by the post office, or in some other way that did not establish its provenance from the German embassy, it would have been difficult to connect Schwartzkoppen with Esterhazy. Without Madame Bastian and the receipt of the document through the voie normale, the indispensable link with Schwartzkoppen, the petit bleu would have become just another piece of mail addressed to Esterhazy complaining about something he had not done right. Given his bizarre personal affairs— unpaid debts, scams, and intrigues—Esterhazy must have received many such letters. This banal letter would not have unmasked him as a spy working for Germany. Inexplicable but surely innocent, Picquart's attempt to alter the petit bleu and conceal the role of Madame Bastian lent itself to future accusations of misconduct, including his having fabricated it, which began to be leveled once his superiors and the Statistics Section turned against him.

There were two other missteps that would confound Picquart: notwithstanding the importance of the petit bleu, Picquart did not tell his direct superior, General Gonse, about it until September 3—and then only because General de Boisdeffre gave him a direct order to do so—and he had not alerted Boisdeffre himself until August 5. Moreover, in subsequent reports he incorrectly stated the date on which the petit bleu had been received, moving it forward in time by as much as six or seven weeks. Failure to report to Boisdeffre sooner can be explained by Picquart's preference for working alone; he wanted to investigate an interesting lead without interference or meddling by his superiors. His not having reported to Gonse at the same time is surely due to the same reason, probably reinforced by the high opinion he had of his own abilities and the considerably lower esteem in which he held Gonse. As for attempting to put a later date on the delivery to the Section of this all-important piece of correspondence, a plausible explanation is that he had belatedly realized that the long delay in reporting to his superiors could open him to criticism, which he tried to forestall by shortening the period between the receipt of the document and his first report. If that was his intention, the maneuver was futile. Gonse was a past master of administrative infighting and had been carefully observing and documenting Picquart's every move.

As one would imagine, Picquart ordered police surveillance of Esterhazy. It garnered little over the summer other than evidence of dissoluteness and irregular financial transactions. The only potential corroboration of the suspicion that he was working for Schwartzkoppen came in the form of a report by a double agent to the effect that until 1895 an unnamed decorated French major had been selling information to the German military attaché. The rank of the officer and his decorations pointed in the direction of Esterhazy. Moreover, the nature of the information the officer was alleged to have been selling to the attaché coincided with matters about which, as Picquart had discovered, Esterhazy had been inquiring of other officers. It is likely that Picquart began to suspect at that time that Esterhazy might be the real author of the bordereau. Such a suspicion would explain the steps he took to obtain specimens of Esterhazy's handwriting. Several came into his hands in the last days of August: letters Esterhazy had been sending to the staff of the minister of war, General Jean-Baptiste Billot, lobbying for a position on the General Staff or at the ministry so as to be able to remain in Paris when his regiment moved from the capital to the provinces. Several photocopies of the bordereau existed in the files of the Section, and Picquart compared the handwritings. The comparison left no doubt in his mind: the document on the basis of which Dreyfus had been accused of treason—and convicted—had been written by Esterhazy, the decorated major who was the real traitor.

Seeking confirmation, he showed the bordereau and Esterhazy's letters to du Paty and Bertillon. Their responses were odd. Du Paty apparently exclaimed that the handwriting on the letters was that of Mathieu Dreyfus; Alfred's and Mathieu's handwritings were in fact very similar. Bertillon said without hesitation that the handwriting on the letters was the same as on the bordereau. However, after Picquart had told him that the letters had been written recently—therefore not by Dreyfus, who was in his cell on Devil's Island—he quickly backtracked and offered as his opinion that the bordereau had been written by someone the Jews had trained to imitate Dreyfus's handwriting.

Picquart took the next step on August 30 or 31. He examined the dossier secret, still kept by the archivist Gribelin in the sealed envelope in which Sandherr had placed it. Picquart's reason for doing so was surely the desire to ascertain whether there was something in the dossier that constituted convincing proof of Dreyfus's guilt independent of the bordereau, evidence that could have justified the judges' finding Dreyfus guilty. It is important to remember that up to that point Picquart had manifestly believed in Dreyfus's guilt. We have seen that he had been aware of the dossier's existence and the use that had been made of it: in fact, it was he who had reported to Mercier and Boisdeffre that knowing it had been given to the military judges after the conclusion of the court-martial hearings had made it possible for him to remain calm. Belief in Dreyfus's guilt is the only plausible explanation for Picquart's not having been shocked by the use of secret evidence: he had assumed that it led to the same conclusion as the bordereau. The difference between the situation then and the one he faced in the summer of 1896 was that he had belatedly realized that the bordereau did not incriminate Dreyfus. Being first and foremost a soldier, he wanted to give the military leaders, Mercier and Boisdeffre, the benefit of the doubt. He did not want to believe that they would have gone forward with the prosecution of the Jew unless there had been adequate proof of his guilt. That proof had to be in the dossier secret, and Picquart wanted to reassure himself by studying it. To his chagrin, he came instead to the conclusion that the documents in the dossier had no probative value. On September 1, he wrote his first official report urging an investigation of Esterhazy. Unfortunately he gave the end of April as the date on which the petit bleu had been received, a misstatement that undercut his credibility and would be used against him.

What followed first was a meeting with Boisdeffre in which Picquart reported on his investigation and advised the general that since the author of the bordereau was Esterhazy and not Dreyfus, and since the dossier secret did not contain any evidence of Dreyfus's guilt, the frightful error committed in 1894 should be rapidly corrected. If it were not, the Dreyfus family would discover the facts, and once it was revealed that the high command of the General Staff had known the truth and had not acted, the army would suffer great harm. Boisdeffre, who had been listening to Picquart in silence, reacted to the mention of the dossier by asking why the documents had not been burned in accordance with the agreement among Mercier, Sandherr, and himself. Picquart had not been aware of that agreement, and he replied that Sandherr had simply told him where the dossier was kept, in the custody of Gribelin. The next day Boisdeffre told Picquart that he had been unable to sleep after what he had been told and ordered him to report to Gonse at Gonse's house in a near suburb of Paris, where he was on leave.

On September 3, Picquart saw Gonse, who heard him out, including the argument concerning the need to take action before the Dreyfus family did. As a first response, Gonse made a face and mumbled, "So we may have made a mistake." In the conversation that followed, Picquart attempted to elicit from Gonse concrete advice that he could take back to Boisdeffre. None was forthcoming. However, Gonse made a suggestion: the two cases, Dreyfus's and Esterhazy's, had to be kept separate. That Dreyfus was the author of the bordereau was *res judicata*—a matter that had been decided by a court of competent jurisdiction—that had to be respected. Consequently the responsibility for the bordereau had to remain with Dreyfus. Esterhazy should be prosecuted for other potential crimes, provided sufficient proof existed. That was the position that Boisdeffre and Billot in due course adopted as well. It boiled down to a preference for having two culprits under key: Dreyfus since his innocence had not been proved, and Esterhazy, if he could be convicted. The situation was delicate: as Gonse put it, "The honor of two generals [Mercier and Boisdeffre] is at stake."[11] So far as Picquart was concerned, he and his superiors had arrived at an impasse.

Picquart and Gonse resumed their dialogue by correspondence some days later without bringing satisfaction to Picquart: the general ordered him to proceed with extreme caution in his investigation of Esterhazy and to report to him on September 15, when he would have returned to the ministry. Pending that meeting, Picquart obtained permission from Boisdeffre to take his story to the minister of war. Billot heard him out with apparent sympathy—possibly inspired by his dislike of Mercier and Boisdeffre—and urged Picquart to continue his investigation while he, Billot, turned the matter over in his head. The next day Boisdeffre asked Picquart how the talk with the minister had gone and criticized him sharply for having told the minister about the dossier secret, an action that he called an attempt to cause dissension among his superiors. Boisdeffre saw Billot himself the next day and in all probability convinced him that reopening the Dreyfus case would be dangerous. From that point forward, whatever impression the comparison of the bordereau and one of Esterhazy's letters may have initially made on Billot, he actively and unyieldingly opposed attempts to obtain a review of Dreyfus's conviction.

Gonse returned to his office as scheduled, on September 15. During the last ten days of his vacation he—as well Boisdeffre, Billot, and the officers at the Statistics Section—had suffered a series of shocks. In addition to the discomfiture caused Boisdeffre and Gonse by Picquart's disclosures and persistence in importuning them, they had read three deeply disturbing articles. On September 8, *Le Figaro* ran the article about the conditions of Dreyfus's imprisonment. What was far worse, on September 9 and September 15 the two articles appeared in *L'Eclair* concerning the communication to the military tribunal of the dossier secret. They also revealed the approximate content of the bordereau. The effect of the *Eclair* articles on the generals, the minister, and the Statistics Section officers was that of a mortar shell lobbed into their midst. As though that were not enough, Gonse received another letter from Picquart, enclosing the second *Eclair* article, in which he promised to look for the sources of the leaks to the press and pointed out, with a touch of self-congratulation, that his concerns about the difficulties the army would face if it did not take the initiative to correct the judicial error were well founded. It was unnecessary for the general to reply to Picquart's letter: they discussed the matter that same morning face to face.

In the course of that conversation—which became very heated—Gonse, obviously irritated by Picquart's continuing, obstinate insistence on the urgent need to deal with the Dreyfus case, put to him the infamous question "What do you care if that Jew rots on Devil's Island?" Perhaps Gonse thought, in spite of everything he should have by then learned of his subordinate's character, that Picquart would draw himself up to attention and signal, by word or gesture, that the subject would not be mentioned again. If that was his expectation, it was disappointed. Picquart continued to argue, insisting on the injustice of keeping an innocent man in prison. He came back to the potential harm to the army if the truth were found out. As Picquart remembered the conversation, at that point the general pointed out that if Picquart did not tell anyone, no one would ever know. Picquart's response was harsh: "What you are saying, General, is abominable. I will not in any event take this secret with me to the grave."[12] For Generals Gonse and Boisdeffre, that remark sealed Picquart's fate.

In addition to being angered by Picquart's recalcitrance, they could not fail to notice that he was troublingly prescient: he had warned his superiors that the truth would come out and the Dreyfus family would take action. On September 18 it did: Lucie Dreyfus sent her petition seeking judicial review to the Chamber of Deputies. The inevitable questions arose. How had Picquart been able to anticipate these developments? Only a small group of officers knew about the dossier secret—Mercier, Boisdeffre,

Gonse, Henry, Lauth, du Paty, and Picquart himself—as well as, of course, Gribelin. Was Picquart the source of the leak that had made the revelations by *L'Eclair* possible? The others were beyond suspicion. Was he a member of the "Syndicate," allied with the Dreyfus family and perhaps even in its pay? A cabal formed composed of Picquart's subordinates: Henry, the intellectually gifted and fiercely anti-Semitic Lauth, Gribelin, and, below them, François Guénée, a police spy expert in producing trumped-up documents and evidence. They had sensed the mood of Boisdeffre and Gonse and took for granted the leaders' determination to keep the lid closed on the Dreyfus case. Picquart's apparent flouting of the generals' wishes was inadmissible; it was contrary to military traditions of silence and discipline and threatened the established order. But even before the confrontations in September 1896, the French diplomat Paléologue had noted that the congenial atmosphere that had prevailed at the Statistics Section during Sandherr's tenure was gone. "You can see that we regret Sandherr," Henry had told him. "That Picquart is a poseur. And if you only knew what a scoffer!"[13]

Personal dislikes and rancor that had nothing to do with Dreyfus added venom to the relations between Picquart and his subordinates. In Henry's case bitterness at having been passed over in favor of an outsider for the top position, which he had thought would be his given his long service, was aggravated by class resentment. Alone among the General Staff officers, he had been promoted from the ranks. Henry had the rough manners and appearance of a trooper, his education was rudimentary, and he knew no foreign languages, which was an impediment at the

Statistics Section. It would have taken a miracle for this son of small farmers not to find Picquart's presence galling. It did not help that, like Picquart, Henry owed his position at the Statistics Section to General de Miribel, who had valued his bravery in battle and discipline as a soldier but had brought in Picquart to succeed Sandherr. Lauth's dislike of Picquart was probably in part a reflection of Henry's, rather than the result of a reasoned judgment or personal grievance. According to Paléologue, Henry's wife, who was much younger than he, was Lauth's mistress, having become such in Lauth's office at the Ministry of War, into which she ventured one day when she came to see her husband and found that he had gone out.[14] Paléologue claimed that the relationship had evolved into one in which Lauth's total loyalty to Henry, except in matters that concerned his wife, was balanced by his intellectual ascendancy over the cuckolded husband. Animosity toward Picquart would not have been the result of intellectual analysis. Gribelin was naturally hostile to anything that threatened the settled order of his personal kingdom: the Section's sacrosanct files had been desecrated when Picquart opened the sealed envelope and debunked the dossier secret. Besides, both he and Guénée would naturally have felt closer to the jovial, backslapping Henry than to a mandarin like Picquart. The attitude of the two generals was no doubt more complex. Certainly Gonse was unlikely to forget, let alone forgive, Picquart's having gone over his head to Boisdeffre. As for Boisdeffre, renowned for his nonchalance, he surely regretted above all having to concern himself again with the Dreyfus case, which he had considered closed, and with the new and unpleasant problem posed by Esterhazy. Once he found it necessary to take action, however, this fervently religious man did not hesitate to make use of the prestige of his exalted position to validate forgeries and perjured testimony.

There is some irony in the circumstance that if Boisdeffre's dearest wish had been realized he would have been removed from the General Staff early enough in 1896 to prevent his having any further role in the Dreyfus Affair. He had wanted to be named ambassador of France to the court of the tsar of Russia, a position for which he thought he was qualified by previous service as military attaché at the French embassy in Saint Petersburg, and his participation in the final phase of the negotiation of the secret military treaty between France and Russia. According to Picquart's biographer Francis de Pressensé this project was thwarted by two monstrous gaffes the general had committed in May as ambassador extraordinary of France to the coronation of Tsar Nicholas II. The first was his insistence on kissing the hand of the tsarina, which was against Russian court protocol. The second, far graver, was his having offered the tsar, before a ball at the French embassy that the tsar had agreed to attend, condolences on the Moscow catastrophe, an allusion to the stampede that had taken place at the customary coronation banquet for commoners held in a meadow outside Moscow. As a rumor spread that there would not be enough beer for everybody, the mob surged, and some fourteen hundred men and women were crushed to death. Thousands more were wounded. In order to make it possible for the French ball to take place, and for the tsar and tsarina to be present during what should have been a period of deep mourning, it had been agreed between the court and the embassy that nothing resembling the words *catastrophe, disaster,* or *condolence* would be uttered. By persisting in his attempt to offer condolences in the face of the tsar's cold and uncomprehending stare Boisdeffre had made himself ridiculous and, therefore, persona non grata.

The solution Generals Boisdeffre and Gonse devised to the Picquart problem was to send him far away from Paris. They hoped that distance from the capital, the Ministry of War, and the "Syndicate" would neutralize him. The difficulty lay in obtaining the minister's agreement. Billot was a temporizer by nature, and Picquart was so distinguished an officer that to dispatch him on what would seem to informed observers a fool's errand entailed some political risk. While Billot vacillated, Picquart continued his investigation of Esterhazy, albeit with little encouragement from Gonse, and sought information about the leaks to the press of which he was himself suspected. Those suspicions were reinforced by the failure of his investigation and the annoying fact that Lucie Dreyfus had petitioned for a rehearing. For their part, the cabal of his subordinates maneuvered, with Gonse's encouragement or at least tacit approval, to supplant Picquart in the day-to-day management of the Statistics Section and spread the rumor that he was neglecting his work in order to pursue his obsession with Dreyfus and Esterhazy. Although Picquart had surely noticed that his position was being undermined, Boisdeffre decided it was time to take a more direct approach. He expressed dissatisfaction to Picquart with his lack of thoughtfulness and prudence. That was the sort of signal that no experienced officer could fail to decipher: it meant that a decision to remove him from the General Staff had been taken. Boisdeffre's initial idea had been to dispatch Picquart on a mission to Indochina, where he had already served. However, when Billot finally yielded, on October 27, and signed the order sending Picquart away, the destination was not as distant as Boisdeffre had desired. Picquart was to inspect, and if necessary reorganize, the intelligence units within the army corps stationed on the eastern and southeastern borders of France. Moreover, his date of departure remained to be fixed.

The realization that his superior officer was not only out of favor but would also leave Paris loosened the restraints that until then had held Henry back from painting him as a security risk. In one of his conversations with Guénée, he found a theme he could use: that Picquart had figured out which documents in the dossier secret had been doctored. Such knowledge in Picquart's possession exposed Mercier, Boisdeffre, and perhaps Gonse to a charge of fraud in connection with the court-martial and raised their potential liability under French criminal law to a new and higher level. The point was not lost on them. Being aware that Picquart had consulted his close friend and lawyer Louis Leblois in connection with legal problems involving the General Staff's use of pigeon carriers, and that Leblois had visited Picquart in his office, Henry also began to build the case that Picquart had divulged military secrets to him. But even Guénée was unwilling at that point to make that accusation. What Guénée did not dare to do, Henry accomplished. He told Gonse that Picquart had communicated secret documents to his lawyer. Gonse's reaction was to stop by Picquart's office and remove the dossier. In itself the action was trivial; Picquart had devoted sufficient time to the study of its contents and no longer needed to consult it. But it was a humiliation that made his position at the General Staff untenable.

While he intrigued, Henry was worrying about how to strengthen the General Staff's defenses. Picquart's out-of-hand dismissal of the dossier had proved to him that although it had served its purpose in 1894 it could not as constituted withstand critical examination. What was needed was a new dossier, assembled according to the 1894 model but greatly strengthened. Its centerpiece would have to be a document in which Dreyfus was named and clearly revealed as a traitor. Such a document would equip the General Staff with the defensive weapon it needed to ward off doubters. Moreover, knowledge that proof of Dreyfus's treachery existed would stiffen the minister's resolve when it came to dealing with Picquart. Since there was no such document, it would have to be created. The task did not daunt Henry. He would fabricate an unrebuttable piece of evidence—it came to be referred as *la massue* (the club)—that from then on could be used to smash anyone who raised doubts about Dreyfus's guilt. It would be made known that the massue existed and was in the General Staff's possession but that because of its nature it could never be shown. To exhibit it would entail the risk of embroiling France in grave diplomatic difficulties. It was an extraordinarily audacious undertaking. The closest Henry came to explaining what went through his mind when he undertook a deception on that scale and put himself in such peril were his words a little less than a year later, after the forgery had been discovered: "I saw that my chiefs were worried; I wanted to calm them. I wanted to put their minds at ease . . . Everything was going badly . . . I said to myself, 'Let's add the sentence that will make everybody quiet.' *Suppose we had a war* in the situation we're in! . . . While if I do this, calm will return."[15]

Being a man of action, he worked over a weekend at home, with occasional assistance from his wife, drawing on documents in the files of the Statistics Section. On a sheet of quadrille paper of the sort Panizzardi, the Italian military attaché, normally used, to which he added the letterhead, taken from the Statistics Section's files, of a letter obtained through the voie normale that Panizzardi had actually sent to Schwartzkoppen, he composed a letter of remarkable linguistic crudeness. He thought that he should make his prose sound like that of an Italian whose French was not perfect, but he had no ear for how someone like Panizzardi might express himself. The result was a text that had no chance of being accepted as genuine by a literate and careful reader:

> J'ai lu qu'un député va interpeller sur Dreyfus. On demande à Rome nouvelles explications, je dirai que jamais j'avais des relations avec ce Juif. Si on vous demande, dites comme ça, car il ne faut pas qu'on sache jamais personne ce qui est arrivé avec lui.

> [I've read that a deputy will be interpellating about Dreyfus. In Rome they ask for new explanations; I will say I never had dealings with that Jew. If they ask you, say like that, because nobody should ever know what happened with him.][16]

The forgery was also crude in one fatal mechanical respect. Henry hadn't noticed that the lines marking off the squares on the two sheets of paper he had used were not of the same color.

On the one on which he had written his text they were pale blue. On the other one, which he had borrowed from a genuine letter that Panizzardi had sent, they were a bluish gray. For anyone who examined it critically and in a good light, the disparities automatically revealed the letter as a forgery. Henry's letter, like the bordereau and the petit bleu, acquired its own name, consecrated in the history of the affair: *le faux Henry* (the Henry forgery). The marvel is that although so much attention was focused on this document, the fact that it was a fake escaped detection for close to two years, until August 1898.

Within the next couple of days, Henry brought his document to the ministry and showed it to Gonse and Boisdeffre, saying it had arrived through the voie normale. Although until then Madame Bastian had always brought documents to the Statistics Section in batches, Henry did not hesitate to report to Gonse that his time she had brought only the one letter. Gonse was fully aware of the significance of such operational details but astonishingly let Henry's anomalous statement about a document of such capital importance pass without comment. He presented it to Boisdeffre, and the two generals dutifully carried the faux Henry to General Billot. They did not, however, show this new flagrant evidence of Dreyfus's guilt to Picquart, who was still in name the head of the Statistics Section, even though after he had absorbed its impact he might have abandoned his quixotic efforts to exculpate Dreyfus. Picquart learned that the letter existed only a week later, when Billot spoke to him of a new document that proved beyond any doubt Dreyfus's guilt. Even then the minister did not show him the letter or tell him anything of its contents. The reason for this peculiar behavior, according to Boisdeffre's testimony at the Rennes court-martial in 1899, was that the minister had decided, in view of Picquart's forthcoming departure and the position he had taken with regard to the Dreyfus case, that it was better not to show him documents relating to it. A more likely reason is that Henry had urged Gonse to keep Picquart away from the faux Henry. There was a danger that would have been clear to Henry: Picquart would challenge the account of how the letter had come to the Statistics Section, even if he failed to discover the forgery.

A strange and unprecedented ceremony took place within forty-eight hours after the presentation of the faux Henry to the generals. First Lauth photographed the letter. This was a function he regularly performed. Then it was copied by hand by Gribelin, who provided also a minute description of the envelope in which it was alleged to have arrived and of the seal on the envelope. That done, Gonse, Henry, Lauth, and Gribelin signed Gribelin's copy in hieratical order, specifying their rank and functions, and certified it as authentic. The copy was then submitted to the minister. In the opinion of the author of *L'Affaire sans Dreyfus*, Marcel Thomas, the certification procedure was the equivalent of a pact concluded by the old guard of the General Staff: with Boisdeffre as their leader, the conspirators would march hand in hand against Picquart and the proponents of judicial review of the Dreyfus case. The pact's strength would be made apparent by the coordinated and probably rehearsed testimony the conspirators gave at Emile Zola's libel trial in February 1898 and the Rennes court-martial in 1899.

Such peace as the faux Henry augured, and that the generals may have thought they had bought by the plan to get Picquart out of the way, was shattered by the publication of Bernard Lazare's brochure and its wide distribution on November 7 and 8. The brochure's title alone, *Une Erreur judiciaire: La Vérité sur l'Affaire Dreyfus* (A Judicial Error: The Truth About the Dreyfus Affair), was a declaration of war. Lazare laid out clearly and convincingly the odious press campaign against Dreyfus provoked by leaks from the General Staff, the irregularities of the investigation conducted by du Paty, the ignoble role played by Mercier, the disregard of the absence of motive, and the misconduct at the trial. He demolished Bertillon's testimony as well as the probative value of the "canaille de D." letter, pointing out that it was inconceivable that the German attaché would have compromised so stupidly a valuable agent. It seemed obvious to the conspirators and the minister that the only explanation for Lazare's clairvoyance was the existence of a channel of communication from the Statistics Section to the Dreyfus family. They did not know and could not imagine that Lazare had other, very different sources: President Félix Faure and Ludovic Trarieux, a former minister of justice.

Assisted by his police spy Guénée, Henry spared no effort in channeling the generals' suspicions toward Picquart. Then came one alarming leak too many: the publication of the facsimile of the bordereau in *Le Matin*. Finding out where its journalists had obtained that document became a priority. Aggressively grilled by Gonse, Picquart, although not responsible for that leak or any other, lost his footing and made himself guilty of minor misstatements.

At about the same time yet another incident occurred which, coming on top of the facsimile imbroglio and rumors Henry was spreading about Picquart's mismanagement of the Section, including overpayment of agents, made clear to Picquart that he must not attempt to delay his departure. An anonymous letter addressed to one of Esterhazy's cronies, written by someone who had tried to disguise his handwriting, warned the addressee that he and Esterhazy would be subject to accusations in connection with the Dreyfus Affair. The crony panicked and got hold of Esterhazy. Seeking protection and not lacking influential acquaintances, Esterhazy forwarded the letter to a well-placed politician, who took it to General Billot and complained on Esterhazy's behalf. Why was he being hounded by the General Staff? Egged on by Gonse, the minister took the letter to be the case of another leak from the Statistical Section and told Picquart that the investigation of Esterhazy had manifestly been compromised. This was yet another signal to Picquart that he must leave. On November 15 and 16, Picquart turned over the leadership of the Statistics Section to Gonse, and took the train for Châlons, where the first unit he was to inspect was garrisoned. In reality it was Henry who assumed command of the Section, and Gonse delivered into his keeping the petit bleu and the file relating to the investigation of Esterhazy. By coincidence, before the change of command had taken place, in a move fraught with great significance for the future course of the affair, Mathieu Dreyfus had blown up facsimiles of the bordereau and letters from Alfred to Lucie that were reproduced on posters and displayed on walls and in news kiosks across Paris.

Although when they said goodbye Gonse had told Picquart paternally, "You will come back to us in December," the generals took steps to ensure that Picquart did not return any time soon.[17] From the northeast border of France he was sent to inspect troops in the Alps. His request to stop in Paris for a few days to pick up personal effects was denied. The mission in the Alps finished, he was ordered to proceed directly to Marseille and from there to Tunisia. Further orders followed, extending his duties to include the reorganization of intelligence operations in Algeria. Gonse tried to lull Picquart by writing him friendly and informal letters in which he as much as admitted his own initial doubts about Dreyfus's guilt, and by sending him grants of cash for expenses, but it did not take Picquart long to figure out the intentions of his superiors. He prepared a written account of the Dreyfus case as he understood it, and while on leave in Paris at the end of June 1897 he deposited it and Gonse's letters with his lawyer Leblois, instructing him to deliver the file in case of his death to the president of the republic. He also explained to Leblois—who until then had apparently never had any doubts about Dreyfus's guilt— the reasons for his own belief that Dreyfus was innocent and Esterhazy the traitor, but without mentioning the petit bleu, which he rather quaintly felt was covered by professional secrecy. Convinced by Picquart, Leblois tried without success to persuade him to make public the facts as he now knew them. Picquart refused; he had no intention of taking the secret with him to the grave, but he did not want to be the accuser of the army he venerated. However, in a concession that in spite of its limitations proved important, he authorized Leblois to reveal the contents of his account of the Dreyfus case to a government official of his choice if he considered it necessary. At the same time, he absolutely forbade Leblois to make contact with Dreyfus's family or their lawyer, or to name Esterhazy to them or anyone else. That task completed, he returned to Tunisia.

Meanwhile, the efforts of the General Staff cabal were proceeding in a fashion that seems both irrational and preordained. That Picquart was the source of leaks, and a dangerous agent of the "Syndicate," had become an article of faith for both Boisdeffre and Gonse, and perhaps even for the more skeptical Billot. Henry, on the other hand, could be counted on to carry out, and indeed anticipate, the generals' every wish. Lauth, Gribelin, and Guénée marched to Henry's drum. Their twofold project evolved rapidly: to develop sufficient evidence to send Picquart before a court-martial and to orchestrate the defense of Esterhazy.

The urgency of the latter task was underscored by a letter received by Billot on October 16, 1897, reporting that the Dreyfus family had identified two officers, one of whom they intended to frame as the real traitor. Their hope was that the one who was denounced would panic and either kill himself or desert, thus furnishing a basis for a judicial review of the court-martial verdict. The letter was signed P. de C, and its author has never been identified. It could have been Henry, although it seems strange that he would have used the readily recognizable initials of du Paty de Clam, especially since du Paty was about to be lured by Gonse into joining the cabal. In the course of that process, Gonse explained to du Paty the necessity of reassuring and coaching Esterhazy, whom he represented as the officer picked out by the

Dreyfus family to be their victim. According to du Paty's recollections, Gonse insisted on the need to protect General Mercier, the former minister of war, who had trusted his subordinates not to reveal that the dossier secret had been delivered to the military judges and laid out the adverse consequences that would follow if public attention were focused on the Statistics Section and its use of secret funds. Gribelin and Henry were to be Esterhazy's other handlers, with Henry in the self-appointed role of master puppeteer. The first step was to alert Esterhazy to the dangers that awaited him. The letter to Esterhazy was probably dictated by Henry to his wife; it was written in a feminine hand and signed Espérance (Hope), and it warned Esterhazy that he was about to be faced with a huge scandal. A certain colonel "Picart" had assembled specimens of his signature and given them to the "Dreffus" family. The letter was sent on October 18 and reached Esterhazy at his wife's property in the country. It so frightened him that he immediately returned to Paris. Esterhazy's attack of panic made it initially easy for the conspirators to manipulate him.

As the cabal's activities continued, they came to include clownish disguises: Gribelin wore green glasses to a meeting with Esterhazy, and du Paty a false beard. Gradually, as he became more self-assured, Esterhazy began to act more consistently with his character, showing contempt for his handlers and spinning out lies and intrigues, some of which may have had as their purpose eventual blackmail of his General Staff benefactors. Abandoning the claim that Jews had imitated his handwriting on the bordereau, he propounded another theory: yes, he had written it, but on Sandherr's orders, as an agent working for him, in order to entrap Schwartzkoppen. The latter theory—that he had worked for Sandherr as a double agent—was rejected forcefully by Henry, who was loyal to the memory of his former chief and did not want him or the Statistics Section besmirched, and Esterhazy did not make full use of it until after Henry's death in 1898. From that point on, it became a version of the affair from which he did not deviate. He embellished on it by claiming in his own memoir of the affair that Dreyfus had been under suspicion for a long time, and the bordereau had served only as a convenient pretext for accusing him: "Rightly convinced of his guilt, [the investigators] took as their point of departure the principle that it was necessary to have concrete material proof, instead of the absolute moral evidence they possessed, and that was the beginning of all the lunacy."[18]

The effort to entrap and incriminate Picquart had begun soon after he left in November 1896 on his ever-expanding mission. In the course of it, Henry resorted to ploys that were stunning in their daring, crudeness, and repetitiveness. The declarations of Guénée and Gribelin designed to show that Picquart had disclosed military secrets to Leblois grew in precision and incriminating detail. But Henry also began to fabricate incriminating missives that would be sent to Picquart, intercepted, shown to the generals, and then added to the files. The first was the famous "Speranza" letter, known as such because of the name with which it was signed (the Italian version of the name he used ten months later in the anonymous letter sent to Esterhazy). Its contents—pure gibberish—could be taken as compromising. Had it been written in code? Dispatched in December, it weighed in

Billot's decision to extend Picquart's mission to include Tunisia. Almost a year later, in November 1897, after an unremitting effort to convince the generals and the minister of war that Picquart was divulging secret information to the Jewish "Syndicate," Henry followed up with two forged cables to Picquart that could be seen as even more incriminating. The first, signed again "Speranza," announced that everything had been revealed. The second, signed "Blanche," asserted that proof had been found that the petit bleu had been manufactured by "Georges"—Picquart's first name. (In fact, Henry had already "worked" on that essential piece of evidence by obliterating "Esterhazy" from the address and then writing it again over the deletion to make it appear that it had initially been forged by Picquart.) For good measure, coached by Henry, Esterhazy addressed an anonymous letter to Picquart warning him that everything had been discovered and advising him to flee. The response of General Billot when this latest production was shown to him was everything Henry could have hoped for. He appointed Henry to conduct a secret investigation of Picquart.

Everything was thus going exactly as the cabal and Esterhazy might have wished. But once again, a deus ex machina intervened. This time the god took the form of a securities trader by the name of J. de Castro, whose professional dealings with Esterhazy had been extensive. He had read the second edition of Lazare's brochure, which included expert handwriting analyses demonstrating that Dreyfus's handwriting was not that of the bordereau, and he had bought a copy of the facsimile of that document. Without hesitation, he recognized the handwriting of his old client, from whom he had received numerous letters that he still had in his possession. Mutual friends put Castro in contact with Mathieu Dreyfus, to whom he showed Esterhazy's letters. A comparison with the bordereau left no room for doubt: the handwritings were identical. This was the climactic moment Mathieu had been waiting for: he had identified the traitor. On November 15, 1897, he denounced Esterhazy to General Billot as the author of the document on the basis of which his brother had been convicted and called on the general to see that justice was done without delay. Made available to the press, the letter created a considerable stir that could not be ignored. Unable to do otherwise, Billot requested General Saussier to open an investigation of Esterhazy. Saussier complied on November 17, putting General Georges de Pellieux in charge. As though Mathieu's denunciation were not bad news enough, Picquart also counterattacked. He sent a letter to Billot lodging an official complaint against Esterhazy, whom he accused of having libeled him by letter and in the telegrams sent to him on November 10.

This may be the moment to ask, before plunging in the next chapter into the bewildering series of legal proceedings that began in November 1897 and continued for the better part of two years, why the high command of the army so stubbornly refused to correct a judicial error. Why did its honor depend on keeping Dreyfus on Devil's Island? The fear of criminal liability may have had some influence, but it cannot have been the major reason: given the fundamentally militaristic temper of the successive governments and the legislature, the threat of prosecution should have been recognized as remote and one that could have been obviated by appropriate assurances from the cabinet. Was it the far more likely loss of prestigious posts, for instance Boisdeffre's position as chief of the General Staff? Were these reasons enough for two generals, Boisdeffre and Gonse, to foment the fabrication of forged documents, to enter into a criminal alliance with the scoundrel that the high command recognized Esterhazy to be, and to embark on a malicious and criminal campaign against Picquart? It seemed to a politician as shrewd and experienced as Blum, and as intimately familiar with the affair, that these were not reasons enough; for him the explanation had to be the presence within the General Staff itself of a traitor in cahoots with Esterhazy and able to direct the other actors. His choice fell on Henry by reason of his protean capabilities as a forger and bearer of false witness, and because of his strategically perfect position as a Statistics Section veteran with the longest record of service there who had gained the complete confidence of Gonse and Boisdeffre. Blum reasoned that Henry and Esterhazy must have been partners in treason; that when the bordereau came into Henry's hands he recognized Esterhazy's handwriting at once and decided to implicate Dreyfus as the scapegoat. Henry understood that the identification of the true author of the bordereau would inevitably lead to the discovery of his own crime.

This explanation is ingenious and tempting, but modern scholarship has not discovered any basis for it. Indeed, it is difficult to believe that Henry would not have burned the document if he had identified the handwriting on the bordereau as Esterhazy's and felt personally threatened—or even if he had merely wanted, against all probability, to protect an officer with whom he had had friendly relations in the past—as soon as he had pieced it together and realized what it was. Blum recognized that there was a more pedestrian explanation: the conspirators were caught in the gears of deception. One lie begets another: having lied once they had to lie again and again, in the hope of concealing the first lie. That still leaves unexplained their unremitting hostility toward Picquart. As Paléologue noted in his recollections of the Rennes court-martial, "A strange thing and one I have noticed frequently, is that Dreyfus is not an object of hatred for the officers; they speak of him with a cold or contemptuous severity, but without anger and sometimes even with pity. As for Picquart, the name alone of that renegade is enough to arouse them; they detest, loathe, and execrate him to the point of fury."[19]

Anti-Semitism had surely been a reason for the alacrity, if not eagerness, with which Sandherr and his colleagues and superiors had reached the conclusion that Dreyfus was the author of the bordereau, as well as for the uncritical push to prosecute him for treason. We do not know whether Gonse, Boisdeffre, or Mercier had any doubts about his guilt after he had been packed off to Devil's Island. If they had no doubts at first, did they or Billot begin to have second thoughts after the petit bleu had been discovered or, if not then, after Henry's confession that he was the author of the faux Henry and his suicide? It is hard to believe that they had none, but their anti-Semitism must have made it possible to sweep troubling thoughts aside and take comfort in the thesis that the honor and well-being of the army—in reality, concern about their own well-being and reputations—required respect for the judgment of the 1894 court-martial. The corollary was that Dreyfus's case must remain closed. They had no instinctive sympathy for Dreyfus, or any of the sense of the solidarity with a brother officer that should have led them to make sure that he was not a victim of judicial error. As a Jew, he was not their brother; he was an unwanted intruder.

The malevolent persecution of Picquart belongs to a rich tradition of reprisals against whistleblowers who have the temerity to expose abuses and violations of law (or for that matter, blunders) committed by government officials for what they see as patriotic reasons. By adhering to moral standards higher than the group's, whistleblowers breach its code of complicity and quickly turn into hated outsiders. The recent cases of U.S. army officers who have been sidelined or have seen their careers broken because they have spoken up against their civilian and military leaders, whether about the conduct of the war in Iraq or the mistreatment or torture of detainees, are as shocking as they are numerous. So are "dirty tricks" played on whistleblowers. An infamous example was the burglary in the summer of 1972 by President Richard Nixon's "plumbers"—a group of former CIA and FBI agents formed under the authority of Nixon's chief of staff—of the office of Daniel Ellsberg's psychiatrist in an effort to find materials that could be used to intimidate or smear Ellsberg. Ellsberg's sin was having given the *New York Times* the Pentagon Papers, which revealed that the Gulf of Tonkin Resolution —the legal basis for the war in Vietnam—had been fraudulently obtained, as well as many other lies that had been told the American people about the war. A recent case of ire directed at a critic of the Bush administration who touched a raw nerve was the vindictive response, especially by Vice President Cheney's office, to the op-ed article "What I Didn't Find in Africa" by former U.S. Ambassador Joseph C. Wilson IV, published in the *New York Times* on July 6, 2003, in which Wilson debunked as unreliable, and probably based on a forged document, claims made by President Bush in his 2003 State of the Union address and Vice President Cheney that Niger had sold yellowcake uranium to Iraq in 1999 to help Iraq's efforts to develop weapons of mass destruction. Within days after Wilson's article and his subsequent appearance on television, the White House spokesman admitted that the State of the Union statement had been in error and confirmed the correctness of Wilson's claims. Nevertheless, one of the byproducts of the administration's displeasure was the outing in the *Washington Post* shortly afterward of Valerie Plame, Wilson's wife, as a CIA operative on weapons of mass destruction. Disclosure of the identity of covert agents is prohibited by U.S. law and could have put Plame in danger. Wilson's ten-day fact-finding mission to Niger in 2002, undertaken at the request of the CIA and at its expense, on which he had based his article was characterized as nothing but a "boondoggle" arranged by Wilson's CIA wife—a boondoggle followed by a report to the CIA that, if heeded, should have at the least have caused serious questioning of a premise on which the attack against Iraq would soon be based.

4 "the truth marches on and nothing will stop it"

As we have seen, after receiving Mathieu Dreyfus's letter denouncing Esterhazy as the author of the bordereau and a traitor, General Billot found himself obliged to take action against the General Staff's new protégé: he ordered General de Pellieux to conduct an inquiry into Esterhazy's conduct. At the same time, in a move charged with black humor, he entrusted to General Gonse a secret investigation of Picquart, taking it out of the hands of Henry, a mere lieutenant colonel. Meanwhile, the minister had to prepare to face disclosures threatened by Auguste Scheurer-Kestner, one of the grand old men of French politics and yet another Alsatian whose patriotism had been inflamed by the loss of Alsace and Lorraine. Jailed under the Second Empire for his opposition to the authoritarian rule of Napoleon III, he was first elected to the Senate in 1872. In 1875 he was made *inamovible* (a life senator) and enjoyed an unchallenged reputation for high-minded probity. The huis clos imposed during the 1894 court-martial had disturbed Scheurer as a matter of principle, and so had rumors about a document having been given to the military judges in secret. He had spoken to friends about his disquiet but, unable to make his mind up concerning Dreyfus's guilt, had taken no action and would have perhaps remained on the side-lines if he had not received, on July 13, 1897, a visit from Pic-quart's lawyer, Leblois. The lawyer had heard about Scheurer's vacillations. Since Picquart had authorized Leblois to reveal what he had been told to a government official if he thought it neces-sary, and remaining silent seemed to Leblois immoral, Leblois turned to Scheurer and disclosed in confidence everything he had learned from Picquart about Dreyfus's innocence and Ester-hazy's guilt. These revelations left out one important fact: as we have seen, Leblois knew nothing about the petit bleu. Moreover, because he feared that by speaking to a senator instead of, for ex-ample, the minister of justice, he might be violating Picquart's instructions, which authorized him specifically to speak to a gov-ernment official, Leblois imposed foolish constraints of his own that were going to hobble Scheurer: he made the senator agree not to reveal that Picquart was the source of the information and not to divulge Esterhazy's name to the Dreyfus family. Moreover, he withheld Gonse's letters.

Scheurer agreed that as a first step he would make it widely known that he had finally come to believe in Dreyfus's innocence based on a file of important evidence in his possession. He also promised to transmit the evidence to the president of the republic or the minister of justice and to demand a judicial review of the 1894 judgment, but only after he had been able to satisfy himself independently that the handwriting on the bordereau was Esterhazy's. For that purpose he needed a suitable handwriting sample. It proved difficult to find. In the end Scheurer obtained one by sending Esterhazy a letter under an assumed name to which Esterhazy wrote a reply. Leblois's refusal to have Picquart named as his source was another problem, inasmuch as withholding it lessened Scheurer's credibility, but as subsequent events proved Leblois was right to fear the dangers to which Picquart would be exposed once his identity became known. The result of these difficulties was that Scheurer mentioned the file of exculpatory evidence so often without revealing its contents, and above all without naming Esterhazy or Picquart, that his admonitions that a monstrous wrong had to be corrected became old news. What was worse, his misplaced confidence in his childhood friend Billot and his old political friend Jules Méline, who was then the prime minister, led him to agree to postpone taking action while Billot was conducting his own investigation. But Billot was not interested in getting at the truth; he wanted only to gain time. When on December 7 Scheurer at last revealed everything he knew about Dreyfus's case on the floor of the Senate, he found that Billot had pulled the rug from under his feet. The minister had spoken in the Chamber of Deputies on December 4 expressing complete confidence in the army and had impressed his audience. Scheurer's speech fell flat. The nationalist and anti-Dreyfusard press, receiving its orders directly from the General Staff, had been smearing his name as a preventive measure since early November, calling him a demented old fool who had been bribed by Jews. The campaign increased in vehemence after Scheurer's speech and proved effective. In January 1898 Scheurer was defeated in his bid for reelection as vice president of the Senate.

Before that, however, in the fall of 1897 Scheurer played, along with Lazare and Leblois, a crucial role in recruiting the great novelist Emile Zola to the cause of Dreyfus's defense. Zola's importance in the phase of the affair that was about to open cannot be overstated. He had always made common cause with outsiders and victims of injustice, and for more than a year he had been appalled by the eruption and spread of vicious anti-Semitism in France. He had spoken out forcefully against it in a long article, "Pour les Juifs," published in *Le Figaro* on May 16, 1896. Without connecting it to the Dreyfus case, he had called anti-Semitism a "monstrosity," and declared himself "stunned to see that such a return to fanaticism, such an attempt to wage a holy war can have occurred in our day, in this great Paris of ours, amid the good people of France."[1] But although he had thought of using the degradation ceremony that Dreyfus had undergone in a novel some day, he had not been following the affair closely and had not even been aware of major developments such as the publication of the facsimile of the bordereau in the fall of the previous year. Leblois had called on him in October 1897 to speak about the case, and the two met again later. Urged by Leblois,

Zola then had lunch with Scheurer, who resolved his remaining doubts about Dreyfus's innocence, and became one of the most determined supporters of Dreyfus's cause.

The insults hurled at Scheurer shocked and disgusted Zola, and he came to his defense in a powerful article, "M. Scheurer-Kestner," published in *Le Figaro* on November 25. Mathieu Dreyfus and Alfred Dreyfus's lawyer Demange had preferred a low-key approach focused on judicial remedies. Zola's instincts told him that this was wrong: the struggle for Dreyfus's exoneration could not be confined to courts of law. He wanted to give *un coup de poing*, "a hard punch," by putting the case before the general public, the widest possible forum, which could be reached only through the press. That is what he proceeded to do. Two more articles appeared in *Le Figaro:* on December 1 "Le Syndicat," in which Zola deconstructed and ridiculed the old wives' tale of a Jewish conspiracy, and on December 5 "Procès Verbal," expressing the hope that a court-martial of Esterhazy would cure the nation and cauterize its wounds, thus putting an end to the barbaric anti-Semitism that was setting France back a thousand years. Thereupon a campaign, mounted by anti-Dreyfusards and right-wing nationalists, was launched calling for readers to cancel their subscriptions; it so intimidated *Le Figaro* that the paper refused to print anything more that Zola wrote in defense of Dreyfus. Unwilling to be silenced, Zola turned to the publisher of his novels, Eugène Fasquelle, and published his next two essays on the affair as pamphlets. In "Lettre à la Jeunesse," which appeared on December 14, Zola addressed students who had staged a vehement demonstration against

Dreyfus in the Latin Quarter, imploring French youth to reject "imbecilic" anti-Semitism and return to French traditions of generosity and justice. He warned that if anti-Dreyfusards continued to suppress the truth, France would become the laughingstock of Europe. "Lettre à la France" was published on January 6, 1898, at the beginning of the year that would mark a turning point in the affair. It mocked the gutter press that was preparing the public for a whitewash of Esterhazy and dared to deny that Esterhazy was the author of the bordereau even though a child looking at it side by side with one of Esterhazy's letters could see that the handwritings were the same.[2]

Before Zola's first article was published, the hearings in the investigation of Esterhazy that General Billot had ordered were held, lasting from November 17 to November 20. General de Pellieux, the investigating officer, took testimony from Mathieu Dreyfus, Scheurer, Leblois, and Esterhazy, among others. With a reputation for honesty that was not matched by his intelligence, Pellieux allowed Boisdeffre and Gonse to manipulate him throughout the proceedings. As a result he came to the astonishing conclusion that Esterhazy was *hors de cause,* that there was nothing to be held against him. On the other hand, Pellieux reported—on the basis of the Speranza and Blanche telegrams fabricated by the Henry-Esterhazy duo and insinuations and accusations by Henry, Lauth, and Gribelin—that Picquart seemed guilty. Therefore he, Pellieux, recommended putting Picquart before a formal commission of inquiry in Paris and interrogating him under conditions of strict secrecy. The theory implicitly underpinning these conclusions was one that had been gaining prominence and would acquire the status of revealed truth for anti-Dreyfusards: Esterhazy was the innocent victim of a plot hatched by the Dreyfus family with the aid of Picquart; the handwriting on the bordereau was a Jewish forgery of Esterhazy's handwriting; and the petit bleu had been forged in whole or in part by Picquart to incriminate Esterhazy in place of the real traitor, Dreyfus. Pellieux disregarded the fact that the only member of the Dreyfus family who knew Picquart was the prisoner on Devil's Island. He did not order expert testimony to determine whether the handwritings on the bordereau and letters known to have been written by Esterhazy were the same. Mathieu's and Scheurer's requests to have Picquart called as a witness in the investigation of Esterhazy were unavailing.

As military governor of Paris, General Saussier received Pellieux's report and forwarded it to General Billot without comment. Billot might have preferred to take no action, but by this time the Dreyfusards were no longer a small band of believers. They had developed into a vocal movement that the government could not disregard with impunity. Moreover, Picquart had written to Billot complaining of new attacks by Esterhazy against him appearing in the press. After consultation with the cabinet, Billot informed Saussier that a further formal investigation of Esterhazy, preliminary to a possible court-martial, had been deemed necessary, and that Picquart had been ordered to return to Paris. This cabinet action was a bad omen not only for Esterhazy but for the General Staff: it increased the risk that public hearings would make it impossible to continue to conceal the transgressions committed in 1894.

Having finished with Esterhazy, General de Pellieux turned his attention to Picquart. The principal charges against him consisted of the coordinated testimony of his former subordinates, Henry, Lauth, and Gribelin, the gravamen of which was a reiteration of the anti-Dreyfusard doctrine: in 1896 Picquart had, in violation of law, given documents from the dossier secret to Leblois and had altered or forged entirely the petit bleu. Each one of Picquart's occasional awkward missteps had been magnified and turned into a weapon against him, especially his fibs about the date of the receipt of the petit bleu and the doctoring he had ordered Lauth to do to make it seem as though the document had been posted rather than found in a wastebasket. The conclusion Pellieux reached was that Picquart had been subject to influences—implicitly those of the "Syndicate"—that had caused his inappropriate behavior, and that a commission of inquiry should investigate whether he should be cashiered for dishonorable conduct or, at a minimum, gross misconduct in service.

While this proceeding was still under way, Count Tornielli, the Italian ambassador in Paris, wrote to the French foreign minister that Panizzardi, the Italian military attaché, Schwartzkoppen's friend, and the author of the "cette canaille de D." letter, intended to denounce as frauds the letters referring to Dreyfus by name or an initial that were alleged to have been written by him. Tornielli proposed that Panizzardi be permitted to testify in France under oath. Boisdeffre was consulted and immediately realized that the documents in both the old and the expanded dossier secret were in danger of being revealed as forgeries. His reply was a brazen but effective piece of nonsense: he claimed that Panizzardi could not be heard as a witness because he was personally interested in establishing a point of view that was contradicted by letters in the files of the General Staff, and that if Panizzardi's testimony were accepted those letters could no longer be used in court either in a case against a former minister of war or in a judicial review of the 1894 judgment. Browbeaten by the general, the cabinet decided not to act on Tornielli's offer.

Except for a public relations setback suffered while Pellieux was investigating Picquart, Esterhazy would have had every reason to be pleased with the turn taken by events. But a certain Madame de Boulancy, Esterhazy's relative as well as a former mistress, who had had the misfortune of lending him a large sum of money that he had not repaid, now decided to take her revenge. Through her lawyer she gave Scheurer access to a sheaf of letters Esterhazy had written to her. They were clearly relevant to proceedings in which Esterhazy's character and credibility were an issue, and Scheurer forced a reluctant Pellieux to make them part of the record of the investigation. At the same time, Mathieu Dreyfus succeeded in persuading *Le Figaro* to run excerpts from the letters on November 18, including a passage that read as follows: "If this evening I were told that I should be killed tomorrow as a captain of the uhlans while sabering the French, I would certainly be perfectly happy . . . I wouldn't harm a little dog, but I would have one hundred thousand French killed with pleasure . . . Paris taken by storm and delivered to the pillage of one hundred thousand drunken soldiers, that is the feast of which I dream. So be it!"[3] Esterhazy had become a hero for anti-Dreyfusards of every stripe. Now the public was given an insight into the sadistic side of his character, his shady financial dealings, and his lack of patriotism. He aggravated his case by protesting that the letter was a forgery, a claim that was demolished by handwriting experts. Nevertheless, at the conclusion of General de Pellieux's investigation, Esterhazy, reassured and guided by his Statistical Section mentors, sent Pellieux a letter, based on a draft that the general himself had helpfully edited, asking for the opportunity to clear his name before a court-martial. He made copies of the letter available to the press. The matter was submitted to General Billot as minister of war. Not having any doubts about the outcome of the trial, the minister was happy to oblige.

A Major Ravary, attached to the military tribunal in Paris, was put in charge of the formal investigation of Esterhazy and held hearings beginning on December 4. On the same day, Billot was questioned in the Chamber of Deputies by one of the leaders of the right-wing parties about the government's position concerning the Dreyfus Affair. The prime minister, Méline, had already spoken, stating that there was no longer any such thing. Billot's reply was more fulsome. He declared, "The Dreyfus case has been regularly and justly decided. . . . As for the odious attacks or accusations that for much too long have been aimed at the leaders of the army and especially its eminent chief of General Staff, I regret from the bottom of my heart that the law leaves me without weapons and I cannot prosecute them."[4] He was acclaimed by the chamber, and an overwhelming majority voted to express confidence in the government and the army, as well as respect for res judicata, the determination of Dreyfus's guilt by the 1894 court-martial. The delay in making his disclosures, which

Billot had wrested from Scheurer, had proved its value, enabling him to neutralize the old man.

Meanwhile, the hearings before Ravary continued. Mathieu Dreyfus remembered Ravary as relentlessly biased against him and Scheurer; he was there to see that Esterhazy emerged unscathed. Ravary's three handwriting experts came to the startling conclusion that the bordereau had not been written by Esterhazy; it merely contained certain words that had been traced onto it from a document that was in his hand. On January 1, 1898, Ravary delivered his report, recommending that the case against Esterhazy be dismissed. The next day, however, General Saussier ordered Esterhazy to stand trial on the ground that not all aspects of the case had been elucidated. Two days later, Picquart filed with the office of the Paris prosecutor a criminal complaint against persons unknown, alleging fraud and libel committed against him through the use of the anonymous telegrams. The move did not shield him from his General Staff enemies. On January 13, he was punished with sixty days' imprisonment at the Mont-Valérien fortress. The formal investigation by a military commission of inquiry that Pellieux had recommended was to follow.

After two days of hearings in the Esterhazy court-martial, conducted almost entirely in huis clos and held in the same courtroom as Dreyfus's court-martial in 1894, on January 11 the military judges, after only a few minutes of deliberation, unanimously found Esterhazy not guilty. The Dreyfus family and Dreyfusards recognized the verdict as a catastrophe. The Dreyfusard press had been arguing for some time, without being able to prove it, that Dreyfus was innocent. When Mathieu denounced

Esterhazy as the author of the bordereau, it became possible to believe that proof of Dreyfus's innocence had been discovered: the universal view among Dreyfusards was that no one who had studied the bordereau and one of Esterhazy's letters closely could doubt that the two documents had been written by Esterhazy. Since the bordereau was the only proof of Dreyfus's guilt adduced at the 1894 court-martial, it was an easy syllogism that once its authorship had been authoritatively attributed to someone other than Dreyfus the government could not refuse to seek a judicial review of his conviction. Now the tables had been turned. By putting Esterhazy on trial and seeing to it that he was acquitted, the minister of war had effectively blocked, perhaps forever, the road to judicial review. He had created a new instance of res judicata, fatal to Dreyfus's case. Dreyfus's guilt had been established by the 1894 court-martial, and now the innocence of Esterhazy had been established by the court-martial just concluded. Could the support of public opinion be maintained in the face of that result? To the feelings of doom was added a dizzying sense of incredulity against which Dreyfus's supporters should have been immunized by what they had learned of the General Staff's ruses. What had made such a result possible, they asked themselves, in spite of the opinions of independent handwriting experts and the testimony of Picquart? The only plausible explanation, but one that was hard to believe by a public conditioned to admire the army and its officer corps, was that the seven military judges had been suborned.

Such was the situation, with Picquart imprisoned in a fortress and Scheurer ousted as vice president of the Senate, when on

January 13 Zola's open letter to President Félix Faure appeared in the left-wing newspaper *L'Aurore*.[5] He had worked two days and all through the night and had produced a masterpiece of political literature. Within a few hours of its appearance more than two hundred thousand copies of the newspaper were sold. Zola's epistle—the extraordinary flair of Georges Clemenceau, the political editor of the newspaper, was responsible for the title "J'accuse . . . !" spread in huge type across page 1—began with a warning to Faure that his name and the name of France had been defiled by the Dreyfus Affair, by the slap in the face of France that was the acquittal of Esterhazy in obedience to orders from above, and by the unspeakable crime of continuing the torment of an innocent man imprisoned for a crime that had been committed by another. From there Zola proceeded to an analysis of the prosecution of Dreyfus and the guilty verdict: the monstrosity of an accusation based on a single document on the authorship of which experts could not agree; the huis clos; the myth of documentary evidence that could not be revealed without a risk of war; the total absence of motive for the crime. Then Zola moved on to Picquart and the petit bleu, correctly inferring that Generals Gonse and Boisdeffre did not doubt that Esterhazy was the author of the bordereau. But denouncing Esterhazy as the traitor ineluctably led to judicial review of Dreyfus's conviction, and that was what the General Staff had wished to avoid at any cost. Therefore, instead of righting the wrong, they had sent Picquart away to a dangerous territory in Tunisia, on a mission that could well have cost him his life. Who is protecting Esterhazy, Zola asked, and answered his own question: Boisdeffre and du

Paty. (We know now that he was right as to Boisdeffre and wrong as to du Paty; his attribution to du Paty of the major role in the conspiracy was an error caused by his not having realized Henry's central importance. Du Paty had been a dupe of Boisdeffre, Gonse, and Henry, rather than an instigator.) A demonstration of the inanity of the accusations directed at Picquart followed: Why would that anti-Semite have manufactured the petit bleu to save Dreyfus and destroy Esterhazy? Could anyone really believe that he was in the pay of Jews?

Finally, Zola put the crucial and prophetic question that would have universal reverberations for military justice: Was it possible to expect that a court-martial would undo what a previous court-martial had done? His answer was no: after the minister of war had proclaimed before the Chamber of Deputies to thundering applause the absolute authority of res judicata, the military judges sitting in judgment on Esterhazy, conscious of the fact that Dreyfus had been convicted by a court-martial, could not give the lie to their predecessors. Zola concluded by accusing du Paty (wrongly), Mercier, Billot, Gonse, and Boisdeffre of being participants and accomplices in the crime committed against Dreyfus, and Pellieux and Ravary of having conducted villainous investigations. Most important for the consequences of his letter, he accused "the first military tribunal of having violated the law by convicting an accused based on a document that was not disclosed, and the second military tribunal of having covered up that illegality, pursuant to an order, by committing in their turn the judicial crime of knowingly acquitting one who was guilty." Zola was courting prosecution for criminal libel, and just in case anyone had missed the point, he cited the relevant provisions of the law and threw down his gauntlet:

> Qu'on ose donc me traduire en cour d'assises et que l'enquête ait lieu au grand jour!
>
> J'attends.

> [Let them dare bring me before the assizes, and let the inquiry take place in the light of the day!
>
> I am waiting.][6]

It is impossible to overstate Zola's courage. As Blum pointed out in his recollections of the affair, Zola had by then reached the summit of his career: in spite of the scandal caused by his many works that had defied convention, notions of good taste, and bourgeois versions of morality, he had won international fame and huge popularity as a novelist; he had become rich; and he had received his share of honors, which he accepted not because they impressed him but because he knew that he deserved them. The only distinction he coveted but had not yet attained was election to the Académie française, and until the publication of "J'accuse" and the scandal it provoked, this had seemed only a matter of time. Nonetheless, after forty years of hard work he had plunged into a new battle, one that would be more fierce than any he had fought before, and had exposed himself not only to public obloquy but to prison, exile, and even assassination.

Bringing a libel action against Zola must have been against the better political judgment of Méline and Billot. They would surely have preferred to rest behind the rampart they had erected of double res judicata and the superficially unbeatable argument that by ordering Esterhazy to be tried by court-martial they had done everything that proponents of judicial review might have desired. Hadn't Dreyfusards been given their day in court? As for the uproar the acquittal had caused at the center and on the left of the political spectrum, it was reasonable to expect that after the passage of some weeks it would die down. That prudent course of action, however, had been made untenable by the furor of right-wing public opinion and politicians provoked by Zola's accusations, and by questions put to the government by the nationalist right in the Chamber of Deputies. Consequently, on January 18, Billot, in his capacity as minister of war, filed a criminal libel complaint on behalf of the military judges in the Esterhazy court-martial, cleverly limiting it to only one of Zola's accusations: that the judges had followed orders when they acquitted Esterhazy. Under French law, truth is an absolute defense in a libel case, but the truth of that particular allegation was, as a practical matter, all but impossible to prove.[7]

Zola's libel trial before the assizes of the Department of Seine, sitting in the Palais de Justice in Paris, began on February 7, 1898, pitting the defendants, Zola and Alexandre Perrenx (the business manager of *L'Aurore*), and their counsel, Fernand Labori and Albert Clemenceau (brother of Georges), against the massed high command of the army, resplendent in full service uniforms, gold braid, and decorations. It continued through February 23. In the background were violent anti-Semitic riots in France and Algeria provoked by "J'accuse." The struggle between the two Frances, one that saw the exoneration of Dreyfus as a moral necessity and one that was outraged by an assault on the honor of the General

Staff inspired and financed by Jews, had never before attained such a degree of violence.

As a matter of law, the question for the jurors to decide was clear—Had the military judges been following their consciences or, as Zola had alleged, orders given by their superiors? The presiding judge tried desperately to confine the questions put by defendants' counsel to this issue, but it was a vain effort. No matter how often he interrupted Labori or Clemenceau with his standard warning that a question put to a prosecution witness was out of order ("la question ne sera pas posée"), the two battered the military witnesses with such skill that as the trial progressed it became clear that the real accused in the dock were Mercier, Boisdeffre, Gonse, and the other General Staff conspirators, together with Pellieux and Ravary. As Léon Blum recalled it, "Zola's essential assertions were shown to be true. . . . The violations of law committed during the 1894 court-martial were proved, which was sufficient ground for judicial review; the absurdity of the attribution of the bordereau to Dreyfus was demonstrated; the General Staff's plot against Picquart was uncovered; the charges against Esterhazy had been marshaled. We had seen, in the flesh and face to face, on one side Picquart, and on the other the 'Uhlan'; all that was left was to evaluate and compare them."[8]

The exasperation of the generals at the grilling to which they were subjected finally reached the boiling point. At the tenth hearing, on February 17, General de Pellieux, having been ruthlessly badgered by Labori, erupted. He asked to be recalled as a witness and proclaimed that there was at the Ministry of War a document that was absolute proof of Dreyfus's guilt. He had seen it and was able to say what was in it: he recited from memory, having consulted minutes earlier with Gribelin, the text of the faux Henry. His testimony caused a sensation. When Labori mellifluously explained that it would be necessary in such a case to bring the document into court and allow it to be examined, Gonse intervened. He addressed the tribunal, urging caution and saying that proof of that nature, which did indeed exist, could not be displayed in public. Not being part of the General Staff cabal, and consequently unaware of the vulnerability of Henry's forgery, Pellieux would have none of it. When the presiding judge suggested that Boisdeffre come the next day to confirm Pellieux's assertions, the general asked his orderly officer to jump immediately into a carriage and fetch the chief of staff.

By the time Boisdeffre arrived, the court had adjourned, and he took the witness stand the next day. His performance was premonitory. Instead of testifying, he addressed the court as follows: "I will be brief. I confirm in every respect the testimony of General de Pellieux as accurate and authentic. I do not have another word to say: I do not have the right. I repeat, members of the jury, I do not have the right! And now, Gentlemen, permit me to say one thing: you are the jury, you are the nation; if the nation does not have confidence in the leaders of its army, in those who have the responsibility for national defense, they are ready to leave that heavy task to others; all you need to do is to speak. I will not say another word."[9] This was to be the paradigm of the General Staff's last-ditch defense: Choose between the army on the one hand and the likes of Zola, the other Dreyfusards, and

Dreyfus himself on the other; dare to declare your distrust of the army; dare to risk the resignation of the army's most eminent generals. The impact of the speech in the courtroom and on the public in general was profound. On February 23, Zola was convicted and given the maximum sentence: one year in prison and a fine of 3,000 francs, a significant sum at a time when, as we have seen, a second lieutenant's pay was less then 2,000 francs.[10] His co-defendant Perrenx was found guilty as well but received a lighter sentence.

Paléologue had not attended the court-martial of Esterhazy, but he was present during many hearings in the libel trial as the representative of his ministry, and he recorded his impressions of some of the principal actors. General Mercier: haughty, phlegmatic, severe, precise, and disdainfully entrenched in the consciousness of his own infallibility; Boisdeffre: distinguished, calm but not stiff, evading dangerous questions with finesse; du Paty: pretentious, with a monocle fixed in his eye and head thrown back, arrogant, a disquieting personage with morbid ideas and a dark and untethered imagination, a strange mixture of fanaticism, extravagance, and foolishness—one would not be surprised to encounter him in one of the fantastic tales of E. T. A. Hoffmann; Henry: thickset, vigorous, massive, ruddy complexioned, with an open face, hiding behind the exterior of rough frankness a good deal of malice; Picquart: slender, distinguished but constrained in his bearing, expressing himself with great precision, visibly troubled by the ferocious hatred of his comrades and perhaps even more by the delirious praise directed at him by the high priests of Dreyfusism, hesitant to choose between what he perceived to be his duty and the risks of open revolt against his superiors.[11]

On February 24, the day after the conclusion of the Zola trial, Prime Minister Méline addressed the Chamber of Deputies and declared that the cases of Zola and Dreyfus had come to an end. It would no longer be possible for those who had tried to keep them alive to claim that they were acting in good faith. If they persisted, they would be pursued to the full extent provided by law; in the event that existing laws proved insufficient, new legislation would be sought. Two days after Méline's speech Picquart was cashiered from the army, the commission of inquiry having found against him 4 to 1.

Zola's conviction was shortly afterward reversed by the Court of Cassation, which held that General Billot did not have standing to file a complaint in a criminal libel action on behalf of the military judges; only they could lodge a valid complaint. Zola was retried beginning on May 23 by the assizes in Versailles, the military judges having duly filed the necessary complaint. A variety of procedural maneuvers prolonged the trial, but on July 18 Zola was once again found guilty. He fled to England, in part to avoid imprisonment and in part to keep the judgment from becoming final. Elections to the Académie française were held on May 26 and again on December 8. Not a single vote was cast for Zola. As for Billot and Gonse, they crowned the successes they had achieved thus far in 1898 by commissioning Billot's son-in-law, a young magistrate, to compile an expanded dossier that included all the principal Henry forgeries and some new ones: trumped-up evidence incriminating Dreyfus that had not been thought of in 1894 but was now added to the file and documents the dates of which had been altered. When completed the dossier contained 375 documents and seemed to Gonse to constitute final and conclusive proof that Dreyfus was a traitor.

Other developments offstage were less favorable to Esterhazy and his General Staff allies. As Mathieu Dreyfus told the story, the trouble began with the complaint alleging fraud that Picquart had filed in November 1897 against persons unknown on the basis of the Speranza and Blanche telegrams sent to him in Tunisia with the intention that they be intercepted and used to incriminate him. An examining magistrate, Paul Bertulus, who was rapidly becoming a Dreyfusard, had been put in charge of the case. It proved to be tangled and difficult, and he made little progress. Coincidentally, early in May 1898 a colleague came to see Labori, who had become Picquart's lawyer, with the story of one of Esterhazy's many scams. (According to Mathieu, these included selling a carriage he did not own, selling a parcel of real estate twice, forging receipts for rent he had failed to pay, not repaying gambling debts run up at his club in Paris or debts to stockbrokers through whom he traded, and adding a zero to the stub of a money order he showed his tailor to persuade him that he had been paid in full.)[12]

In this particular swindle Esterhazy had gotten in touch with the widow of a cousin residing in Bordeaux and her son, Christian Esterhazy, and offered to help them with their finances. His specific proposal was to place 35,000 francs of their funds, which represented substantially all of their fortune, at the Rothschild bank, which he told them would pay interest at the rate of 25 percent per annum. The reason for this favorable treatment was his friendship with a lycée classmate, Baron Edmond de Rothschild. He also suggested that Christian come to Paris, where he would introduce him into the banking milieu. The mother and the son swallowed the bait: they sent the money, and Christian came to Paris. But when Esterhazy's sordid financial dealings came to the surface during Zola's trial, the two became concerned and decided to withdraw their money. Unfortunately, Esterhazy had spent it; there was no Esterhazy account at the Rothschild bank. The victims sought legal advice, and their lawyer put Christian in touch with Labori. The story behind the story was that Christian had been Esterhazy's confidant at the time the Speranza and Blanche telegrams were sent to Picquart, and he was able to explain how the plot against Picquart had been carried out by Esterhazy and Henry. After complicated negotiations, Christian agreed to tell what he knew to Bertulus and filed a complaint for fraud against Esterhazy that came close to putting Esterhazy and his mistress in jail. They were saved by the interference of Bertulus's anti-Dreyfusard superior. Nonetheless, on August 24 a military commission recommended that Esterhazy be cashiered for habitual misconduct. He fled first to Belgium and from there to England.

Meanwhile, the French legislative elections had taken place on May 8 and 22. Having lost support, the Méline government resigned on June 15. After a longer than usual interregnum, it was succeeded on June 28 by a government formed by Henri Brisson, who took as his minister of war Godefroy Cavaignac, a fervent nationalist, a grandson of a member of the convention that voted to behead Louis XVI, and the son of the general who had brutally put down the Paris insurrection of June 1848. Convinced of Dreyfus's guilt and of the existence of a Jewish Syndicate that was plotting against France, Cavaignac was a fierce opponent of judicial review of Dreyfus's case. He did not intend his opposition to be passive; he proposed to take stern measures to clean house. One of his first steps was to ask Boisdeffre whether the authenticity of each document in the dossier secret had been carefully verified; Boisdeffre replied that "the authenticity of the ensemble and the unlimited confidence he had in Lieutenant Colonel Henry seemed to him to be sufficient guaranties."[13] Not content with that statement, Cavaignac commissioned a review of Dreyfus's alleged confession in January 1895 and of the entire reconstituted dossier by two of his close assistants, one of whom was Captain Louis Cuignet.

The tale that Dreyfus had confessed his guilt directly before the degradation ceremony had been gaining adherents. Its origin was a story told by Captain Charles-Gustave Lebrun-Renault of the Garde républicaine to a group of fellow revelers at the Moulin Rouge on the evening of January 5, 1895, the day of the degradation. Lebrun was the officer who had escorted Dreyfus that morning to the Ecole militaire. In Lebrun's account Dreyfus had confessed to him during the time they were together, declaring: "I am innocent. If I have delivered documents to foreigners it was in order to bait the hook and get from them others that are more important; in three years the truth will be known and the minister himself will reopen my case."[14] The story was improbable, given Dreyfus's obstinate refusals to admit his guilt, as reported on several occasions by du Paty, and his demeanor while in prison and during the degradation ceremony, and it indeed was nothing more than loose talk by an officer out to have a good time and to make himself interesting. But one of the revelers was a journalist, and the canard was published the next day in the press. Lebrun was promptly interrogated by the president of the republic and Mercier, and backed away from his story. The confession was disavowed the next day by the government in a *démenti* responding to the articles in the press. Nevertheless, the canard was revived and reinvigorated in 1897, when the General Staff was once again preparing for battle to bar the way to judicial review, and it became one of the persistent themes of the anti-Dreyfusard argument. To make certain that he could rely on Lebrun's initial account, Cavaignac personally interviewed him and felt reassured when the officer showed him a page of his diary in which he had recorded the conversation on the day of the degradation. That diary page was never seen again; the officer later claimed that he destroyed it after he returned home. Since Boisdeffre knew a great deal about the truth of the matter, which was that Dreyfus had never stopped insisting on his innocence, his failure to warn Cavaignac was another instance of his perfidy.

The government was to be questioned again in the Chamber of Deputies about the Dreyfus Affair by an ultranationalist deputy. Cavaignac decided he would make this the occasion of a major speech demonstrating Dreyfus's guilt and the inanity of the attacks on the 1894 guilty verdict: its centerpiece would be the faux Henry. The speech was delivered on July 7. Astonishingly, Cavaignac read in full the faux Henry and two other Panizzardi letters from the dossier secret, including the letter that referenced "that swine D." The speech was a triumph, and the chamber voted overwhelmingly, with only two votes against and sixteen abstentions, to have it reproduced on posters that would be displayed across France. Among those abstaining was Méline, who probably knew how little those three documents were worth. Paléologue, who had recently come to believe that Dreyfus was innocent, recalled the July 7 session of the chamber as pathetic. He had no illusions about the value of the Panizzardi letters or the integrity of the faux Henry—he had told the Minister of Foreign Affairs that it stank of forgery.[15] Indeed, two days later Picquart sent a letter to the prime minister asserting that he was in a position to prove that there was no connection between Dreyfus and the two Panizzardi letters from 1894 and that the third, the faux Henry, was a forgery. His letter was published in a Paris newspaper, *Le Temps*. Cavaignac's riposte was to file a criminal complaint against Picquart and Leblois, alleging that Picquart had given Leblois access to military secrets. The next day Picquart was arrested and jailed at the Santé prison in Paris. Cavaignac also proposed that the government prosecute a large number of persons—leading Dreyfusards—for conspiracy and sedition. For good measure he ordered that Esterhazy be arrested and appear before a commission of inquiry to determine whether he should be discharged from the army on the ground of habitual misconduct. Esterhazy, who had not yet been confronted by his cousin Christian, was still in Paris.

The effect on Dreyfusards of Cavaignac's speech and its reception by the chamber was devastating, its impact increased by Cavaignac's reputation for honesty and thoroughness. No one could suspect him of conniving with Boisdeffre or Gonse. This was a catastrophe as great as the acquittal of Esterhazy at his court-martial six months earlier. Moreover, if Cavaignac was right and the documentary evidence proved Dreyfus's guilt, it could also be taken to prove the anti-Semites' and anti-Dreyfusards' new thesis, that Esterhazy was an innocent victim whom the "Syndicate" had attempted to substitute for the real traitor, Dreyfus, and that Picquart was an agent of the Syndicate and had forged the petit bleu. But just as Zola had broken with his "J'accuse" the evil spell cast by Esterhazy's acquittal, another powerful voice, that of Jean Jaurès, the socialist leader, would in short order reveal the defects in Cavaignac's exposé. Blum recalled Jaurès's arrival at his apartment, where he and a group of friends were commiserating with one another about Cavaignac's speech. Jaurès told them to cheer up: for the first time, he said, our victory is assured: "The counterfeiters have come out of their hole, we have them now by the throat. " And indeed, a day later he published in his newspaper, *La Petite République,* an open letter to Cavaignac in which he announced his plan of battle: he would refute one by one every element of proof Cavaignac had advanced in his speech. He proceeded to do just that in a series of articles that ran in *La Petite République* through August and September and were republished in book form as *Les Preuves* (The Proof).[16] Taken together, they constitute another masterpiece of political literature. By the time Jaurès had finished, there was nothing left of the anti-Dreyfusard argument that had not been demonstrated to be beyond the pale of rational discourse.

The fundamental question Jaurès put forward was whether, as he maintained, the faux Henry was a forgery produced within the General Staff, that Holy Ark of the French army. If that was the case the General Staff's prosecution of Dreyfus had opened a bottomless pit of infamy. The answer came on August 13. Working alone at the Ministry of War, Captain Cuignet examined closely the faux Henry in the light of a lamp and noticed the disparities that revealed it as a forgery. They were not as apparent in the daylight. He advised Cavaignac of the forgery the next day, but two weeks passed before the minister took any action: he did not report Cuignet's discovery to the prime minister or to Boisdeffre or to the prosecutor in charge of the case against Picquart, although that proceeding was based solely on allegations by Henry and his subordinates. "It must really be, as Brisson, who will never forgive him his silence will say, that Cavaignac had been 'hypnotized' by his hatred for Picquart and the 'Syndicate' to have kept silent for fifteen days about what he had just learned." An additional force at work was Cavaignac's blind certitude that Dreyfus was guilty. According to his logic, the discovery of the forgery did not invalidate the judgment of the 1894 court-martial because the date of the faux Henry was posterior to it. It could be disregarded. However, as minister of war he had to deal with Henry. On August 30 he interrogated Henry in the presence of Boisdeffre and Gonse. Henry admitted the forgery and was imprisoned at the fortress of Mont-Valérien, where Picquart had been jailed because of Henry's plots against him. The next day he slit his throat with his own razor. Boisdeffre resigned from the army as soon as Henry had signed his confession. Shortly thereafter, Gonse was transferred to a line unit command, and on September 12 du Paty was retired from the army at half pay. The response of the politically uncommitted press to Henry's confession and suicide and Boisdeffre's resignation was to declare itself in favor of judicial review of the Paris court-martial's conviction. A majority of nationalist and anti-Semitic newspapers bowed, however reluctantly, to the apparent necessity of such a move. Dreyfusards rejoiced in the belief that judicial review had become inevitable.[17]

When told of Henry's suicide, Prime Minister Brisson, who appears to have come over to the Dreyfusard side, reportedly exclaimed: "Now we will have judicial review![18] On September 3 he asked a mutual friend to advise Mathieu Dreyfus that this was the moment to seek it, and Lucie Dreyfus's petition was delivered that evening. But Brisson had not taken into account the vehemence of the anti-Dreyfusard passion of Cavaignac or within the army. Cavaignac would not agree to the government's sending a request to the Court of Cassation, thus forcing Brisson to ask for his resignation. General Emile Zurlinden, whom Brisson named to succeed Cavaignac, at first seemed ready to accept the necessity of review; in fact he had asked his colleague the minister of the navy to send a vessel to the Salvation Islands to be ready to bring Dreyfus back to France. But he changed his mind abruptly, claiming that judicial review was impossible, and resigned eight days after taking office. The aggressive opposition to review of the former minister of war and a senior general notwithstanding, the Dreyfusards' political situation had changed prodigiously: Mathieu recalled that Brisson consulted him about finding an appropriate candidate to replace Zurlinden. The general Mathieu recommended—he had presided at Dreyfus's degradation ceremony and was said to have been deeply affected by it—was unwilling to accept the appointment. Ultimately, the hapless prime minister was able to recruit General Charles Chanoine, who acquiesced in seeking the review, clearing the way for the minister of justice to file at long last the government's request with the Court of Cassation on September 26, 1898, almost exactly two years after Lucie first petitioned the Chamber of Deputies. One month later, on October 26, the court ruled that the government's request was receivable as to form and ordered a full investigation into the merits of the 1894 court-martial's judgment.

In the meantime, as though neither Henry's suicide nor the departure of Cavaignac and Boisdeffre had happened, the prosecution of Picquart was going forward. He had been imprisoned since July 13 awaiting trial before the Paris assizes on the charge of disclosure of secret documents to Leblois. His court appearance in that case was scheduled for September 21, and his chances of having the case dismissed or at least being provisionally released from jail seemed to be good. But that day, General Zurlinden, who had returned to his old post as military governor of Paris (previously occupied by General Saussier), took an unimaginable step: he signed an order accusing Picquart of having forged the petit bleu, a crime punishable by court-martial. At the request of the prosecutor, the court decided that the ordinary criminal case (disclosure of secret documents) would be suspended while military justice pursued its course. Thus, having spent 72 days at the Santé common-law prison, Picquart was transferred the next day to the military prison on rue du Cherche-midi, where he was held in solitary confinement. He was allowed to see Labori for the first time on November 13. At that point he had been imprisoned 122 days, 49 of them incommunicado.

It took a series of complex procedural maneuvers to remove Picquart from the grasp of the military. On March 3, 1899, the Court of Cassation ruled that the acts of which he stood accused all related to the common-law proceeding pending against him and Leblois, and ordered his release from the military prison. That decision did not mean, however, that he was set free. He returned to the Santé prison and remained there until June 9. On July 13, ten days after the Court of Cassation had overturned the 1894 verdict and the day Alfred Dreyfus started his return voyage to France, all charges against Picquart were dismissed.

Even more astonishing, if possible, than the continued persecution by the military of Picquart was the apotheosis of Henry then in the making. Rumors spread that he had been assassinated at Mont-Valérien by Jews afraid of revelations he might make. The faux Henry was transformed into *le faux patriotique,* the forgery that the heroic colonel had fabricated in order to save his country. In December 1898 a subscription was opened for a fund for his widow and orphaned son, intended to make it possible for them to defend Henry's honor by bringing a libel action against Joseph Reinach, who had accused Henry in writing of having been Esterhazy's accomplice in treason. More than 130,000 francs were raised in less than a month, amid an orgy of anti-Semitic insults and calls for the massacre of French Jews. Among the donors were three thousand officers and twenty-eight retired generals, including General Mercier, seven dukes and duchesses, and almost five hundred marquises, counts, viscounts, and barons, as well as a handful of leading intellectuals, including the great poet Paul Valéry and a less great poet, Pierre Louÿs, who was then in vogue.[19]

The investigation of the 1894 court-martial by the criminal chamber of the Court of Cassation was intensive and stately, and conducted with the utmost respect for the law, but along the way it fell victim to the extraordinary politicization of the court. A grandstanding, attention-seeking judge—who subsequently resigned to become a journalist—accused the chamber of both gross partiality or worse toward Dreyfus and Picquart and disrespect for the army. These charges, appropriately embroidered upon, led to violent agitation, with anti-Semites openly accusing Jews of having corrupted the court, as well as to poisonous personal attacks in the press against leading judges. The resulting impasse was solved by the passage on March 1, 1899, of a law stripping the criminal chamber of jurisdiction: it was permitted to complete the investigation but after that the case would be heard by all the chambers of the court sitting together *en banc,* as a united chamber. The new law aroused feelings of indignation even in an observer as detached and ironic as Paléologue: "This departure from all rules of procedure, this arbitrary incursion of political power into the domain of justice is too scandalous to bring about the least appeasement."[20]

The criminal chamber's investigation had in fact been completed when the law was passed, and its report was transferred to the united chamber, which, perhaps in order to show that it did not intend to rubber-stamp the criminal chamber's findings, demanded the testimony of more witnesses and ordered an additional investigation. The suspense surrounding the eventual decision was intense. At this point, Mathieu Dreyfus made a remarkably astute move, comparable to his having asked for Bernard Lazare's assistance in seeking support for the cause: with the help of the lawyers, Mornard and Labori, he found a way to skirt the legal prohibition against the reproduction and publication of transcripts of hearings before the criminal chamber before they were read in open court. The scheme may have been illegal but it proved effective, and there was no prosecution of Mathieu or the lawyers. *Le Figaro* began publication on March 31, and by the end of April it had published the entire set. As a result an important segment of the public became acquainted in great detail with the crimes committed in 1894 to secure Dreyfus's conviction, and the reversal of the Paris court-martial verdict assumed an air of inevitability. The Court of Cassation's judgment was read on June 3, 1899. The legend of Dreyfus's confession was discredited in the recital of facts (*attendus*). The court did not consider the faux Henry since it had had no role in the conviction of Dreyfus in 1894. "La canaille de D." was deemed not to refer to Dreyfus. The court found that the bordereau had not been written by Dreyfus, but no opinion was expressed about its authorship. The judgment of the military tribunal was overturned, and Dreyfus was sent back for a new trial by court-martial. This was what his lawyer Mornard, with Lucie's and Mathieu's agreement, had requested. The question for the court-martial would be, "Is Dreyfus guilty of having in 1894 practiced machinations or entered into understandings with a foreign power or one of its agents in order to induce such to commit hostile acts or undertake a war against France, or in order to procure for such the means thereof by delivering the memoranda and documents referred to in the above-mentioned bordereau?"[21] Even if Mornard had not asked for a new court-martial to give Dreyfus the opportunity to clear his name before a tribunal of his military peers, it is doubtful that in the highly tense political situation a reversal without remand for a new trial could have been obtained.

The censorship of Dreyfus's correspondence imposed by the Ministry of Colonies was so severe—and so malevolent—that Alfred Dreyfus knew nothing of Mathieu's and Lucie's efforts to wrest from the government the review of his conviction or of their successes beginning in September 1898. All he knew was that his own petitions for review and other appeals to the government had gone unanswered. Unexpectedly, on October 27, 1898, he received notice from the prison authorities that he was going to receive "a definitive answer to his request for review addressed to the head of the state." A letter from Lucie, sent in September, arrived a few days later, reporting that events of grave importance had taken place and that the government had accepted her petition seeking review. But no one told him whether the court had accepted it, and he had no inkling of the developments to which Lucie alluded. At long last, on November 16, a telegram from the commandant of the Salvation Islands advised "deportee" Dreyfus that the criminal chamber of the Court of Cassation had accepted the petition and he was "invited to produce his defense."[22]

The regime to which he was subject now changed slightly: he was authorized to be outside his cell for longer hours and to move about within the enclosure that surrounded it, a sort of circular corridor without shade, from which for the first time since the fall of 1896 he could see the ocean and the meager vegetation of the islands. No letters from Lucie reached him until December 18, when he received one dated November 22 that referred to other letters she had written, none of which had been transmitted to him, and to a letter from him in which he had apparently expressed the intention of not writing again, even to her. Not having intended any such thing—as it turned out, a passage taken out of context from one of his letters had been cabled to Lucie—he wrote to express his outrage to the governor of Guiana: "By sending to Mme Dreyfus only an excerpt from my letter an interpretation has been given which must have been more than painful for my dear wife."[23] One has to admire the spunk that made it possible for this man, after more than four years of solitary confinement, to berate a high government official and refer to his wife as Madame Dreyfus as if he were still living on the chic avenue du Trocadéro.

In the last days of December he received the opening statement by the government's counsel in the criminal chamber proceedings, as well as pen and paper with which to take notes. A series of mind-boggling events was revealed to him: the denunciation by Mathieu of Esterhazy, a man he had not known existed; the fabrication of the faux Henry; Henry's confession and suicide. At the beginning of the new year, on January 5, 1899, Dreyfus was interrogated by the president of the Court of Appeal of Cayenne pursuant to an order of the Court of Cassation and was shocked to hear that his vehement protestations of innocence on the day of degradation had been twisted into a confession of guilt. Then for many months all was again silence. Not knowing about the furor that had resulted in the stripping of the criminal chamber's jurisdiction, he could not understand the delays; his case still seemed to him simple, a matter of determining whether he was the author of the bordereau.

The news came at half past twelve on the afternoon of June 5. The chief of the guard detail rushed into his cell and delivered a memorandum stating that the Court of Cassation had reversed the military tribunal's judgment and remanded him for a new court-martial in Rennes. He was no longer a deportee: the guards were to be replaced by gendarmes. A navy cruiser, the *Sfax*, was leaving port for Devil's Island and would bring him to France. This time his material situation changed radically for the better. In the evening the prison guards departed, the regime of silence was over, the mayor of Cayenne sent him a suit, a hat, and some linen; and although he was still under arrest, he could think that he was once again a French officer. On June 9, a prison launch conveyed him to the ship. A noncommissioned officer's cabin had been gotten ready for him, with bars blocking the porthole. "Out of a feeling of personal dignity," he wrote, "I spoke to no one except as required by military duty."[24]

On June 30 they came within sight of the French shore, and

the ship stopped its engines. "After five years of torment," Dreyfus remembered thinking, "I was returning to seek justice." The disillusionment, the first sad and painful impression, came quickly. The *Sfax* received orders to lie offshore under steam; in the afternoon it maneuvered slowly along the coast, and at about seven in the evening the engines stopped. It was a black night, with fog and gusts of rain. At nine, Dreyfus was asked to descend the ship's ladder and board a launch that was bobbing up and down on the heavy seas. He fell, injuring his leg painfully. An attack of fever—he was to suffer from it for the rest of his life—made his teeth chatter. At last they reached a steamboat, which soon got under way. At a quarter past two in the morning they reached land. He disembarked and was transferred to a carriage. A captain of gendarmes and two of his men accompanied him. At the railroad station, he and his escort walked between two columns of soldiers with weapons at the ready. They reached Rennes, the capital of Brittany and a garrison city, after two more hours of travel. Again a carriage was waiting, which took him and the gendarmes to the courtyard of the military prison. It was six in the morning on July 1, 1899. Three hours later, he saw Lucie. Intimacy was out of the question: an infantry lieutenant was on duty in the visitor's cell adjoining the cell in which he was confined. He was to be present each time Dreyfus received a visit.[25]

The court-martial hearings began on August 7. During the weeks preceding the trial and its twenty-nine grueling sessions, Dreyfus gave proof that neither his memory nor his capacity for concentration and analysis of complicated materials had been impaired by the years of imprisonment and solitary confinement. He had mastered the record of his case.

On September 9, after deliberating for one and a half hours, the military judges returned their verdict: by a vote of 5 to 2, guilty with "extenuating circumstances." The sentence imposed was ten years' imprisonment. The next evening, the military judges met again and unanimously agreed that they did not want Dreyfus to be submitted to a second ceremony of degradation and asked that their wishes be submitted to the president of the republic. Degradation was the part of the punishment Dreyfus had feared most; he had told his brother he would not survive it. How had the tribunal reached its absurd verdict, treason with extenuating circumstances? Manifestly, once they had voted, the judges were horrified by what they had done.

The prime minister, Pierre Waldeck-Rousseau, and the minister of war, General de Galliffet, were both convinced that Dreyfus was innocent and had hoped for his acquittal. What had gone wrong? The counsel presenting the government's position at the court-martial could have been instructed to seek acquittal. Instead, Galliffet had allowed him to operate without marching orders, which led to his coming under the influence of the massed group of generals and other high-ranking officers who were bent on obtaining a guilty verdict. Clearly, Dreyfus's defense team had not made sufficient efforts to focus the trial as closely as possible on the one question that had been delineated by the Court of Cassation: Did Dreyfus in 1894 commit treason "by delivering the memoranda and documents referred to in the . . . bordereau" to a foreign power? That the court's formulation was imprecise had not made the task easy. But the trial had meandered disastrously: having been disposed of by the court, the issue of Dreyfus's alleged confession should not have been raised, and the Panizzardi letters should not have been allowed to be mentioned since they too had been eliminated by the court. But they had been produced, together with, to quote Paléologue, wads of paper "in which there are not twenty lines that apply really to Dreyfus. The whole secret dossier of the intelligence service consists of nothing more than apocryphal or touched-up documents, inaccurate translations, twisted testimony, foolish or made-up gossip, scraps of paper arbitrarily put together that like the writings of the Sibyl can be given any meaning one wants, insignificant notes in which one discovers a profound and cabalistic meaning; and that was the entire dossier secret of the Statistics Section."[26] Close analysis should have made it possible to convince the tribunal of their nullity.

The truth is that no one accustomed to the rigor of a U.S. or British trial, with its insistence on the relevance of evidence proposed to be introduced and its abhorrence of hearsay and expressions of opinion by witnesses unless they are testifying as experts, can see the Rennes trial as anything other than an aberration that was certain to produce an irrational result. The assessment of a contemporary Anglo-Saxon observer of the trial, Lord Russell of Killowen, Britain's lord chief justice, as set out in his report to Queen Victoria was mordant: "The explanation of the erroneous judgment, as I conceive it to be, at which [the judges] arrived I take to be this: they were unversed in the law, unused to legal proceedings, with no experience or aptitude to enable them to weigh the probative effect of testimony; they were steeped in prejudice and concerned for what they regarded as the honour of the army and thus, impressed or overawed by the heads of their profession, they gave weight to the flimsy rags of evidence which alone were presented against the accused man."[27] The judges' inexperience, which had weighed so heavily in the conduct of the proceedings, had been aggravated by the failure of the army command to provide them with legal advisers.

Paléologue described a conversation with two of the military judges who had come to see him privately to ask his opinion. Did he think that Dreyfus was guilty? Stiff and proper, Paléologue complied, telling them that he believed Dreyfus to be innocent, and proceeded to coach them on points of particular interest they should try to elucidate, including the following: How had the bordereau gotten from the German embassy to the Statistical Section? Did any facts support the nonsensical myth of the "imperial bordereau," marked up personally by the kaiser, which according to persistent rumor had come into the General Staff's possession and conclusively incriminated Dreyfus? What had been Boisdeffre's and Gonse's opinion of Dreyfus's guilt at the time when Henry decided to fabricate his forgery? Quite apart from the question whether Paléologue was giving those officers good advice, their consulting with the representative of the Foreign Ministry out of the hearing of the accused and his counsel was a serious violation of Dreyfus's rights. There were other such incidents involving Paléologue. On one occasion he was asked by the judges for his opinion of Lauth. Paléologue expressed his contempt, saying that Lauth was the only officer on the General Staff with whom he had broken off all personal relations. The president of the tribunal questioned him separately about the "imperial bordereau." Paléologue's reply was a question: Did he have to deny such crazy stuff? Of course no such document existed. Yes, it was necessary to respond, the president assured him, so that he could deny it to others, whom Paléologue reasonably understood to be the other judges. In addition, Paléologue learned from the director of the Sûreté générale that the closing statement of the government's counsel, succinct and surprisingly effective—and damning for Dreyfus—had not been prepared by that habitual blunderer but instead by one of Mercier's friends, an able nationalist lawyer who, at the general's request, had prepared the pleading and had sent it to the government's counsel.[28] The director had obtained knowledge of this maneuver through an indiscretion of the messenger to whom the closing statement had been entrusted. Not surprisingly, it reflected Mercier's views, not the government's.

Moreover, the defense suffered from three crippling handicaps. First, there was visible dissension, if not animosity, between Dreyfus's lawyers, Demange and Labori. The former was cautious, and in his closing argument he was willing to settle for raising sufficient doubt in the judges' minds about Dreyfus's guilt to prevent a guilty verdict. Labori, a firebrand who had no qualms about berating the army, wanted to insist on the judges' obligation to recognize the innocence of the accused. Second, the effect on the military judges of the army's top brass—five former ministers of war, a former chief of the General Staff, countless generals and colonels—enthroned in the courtroom and proclaiming Dreyfus's guilt was necessarily overwhelming. One could not expect the seven military officers—all of them, to be sure, graduates of the Ecole polytechnique and manifestly intelligent and attentive to the proceedings—to resist being swayed, if not browbeaten, by those leaders of the army, the high priests of its Holy Ark. Their influence was magnified by the presiding judge's attitude and rulings. As Dreyfus put it in his memoir, in that courtroom "truth had the weight of the number of stripes on the sleeve of the uniform." Mathieu recalled that whereas witnesses for the prosecution were given great latitude to develop their testimony and to intervene in the proceedings as accusers, the treatment by the president of the tribunal of witnesses for the defense was brutal. "The guiding spirit," Paléologue wrote, "of the nationalist party is General Mercier. He has installed himself in a modest house that belongs to his retired old friend, General de Saint-Germain. It is there that every afternoon and every evening the defenders of the army meet, first the crowd of military witnesses, then Cavaignac [and leading nationalists and anti-Semites], finally the Breton gentry and many ecclesiastics. It is from here that orders of the day emanate; it is here that the next day's testimony is fabricated and coordinated. General Mercier makes strict discipline reign in the entire camp."[29]

Third, Dreyfus was a terrible witness and an unappealing defendant. This is how Lord Russell, who was clearly predisposed in his favor, described him to Queen Victoria: "I was full of pity for him and entered the Court with every desire to be impressed by him; but I was not. He does *not* impress one favorably. He is mean-looking, with a hard, unsympathetic face; and, so far as expression goes, I must reluctantly admit that there was no openness, frankness or nobility in his expression. He did, I think, display a great deal of dignity in the passionless immobility with which he, almost through the entire proceedings, listened to the injurious and, as I believe, often lying statements launched against him."[30] Every lawyer who has had to face a tribunal knows that the credibility of a witness is a matter of intangibles. A doubt as to his character and veracity raised by the witness's demeanor is all but impossible to expunge.

Paléologue's descriptions of Dreyfus in the Rennes courtroom throw more light on this failing, which plagued him throughout the affair. As Dreyfus heard the 1894 indictment read aloud, Paléologue saw huge tears fill his eyes and flow down his cheeks. But immediately afterward, his face became again an impassible mask, a "poor worn mask, etched by sorrow." He responded to the president of the tribunal in a dry, uneven monotone. When the president questioned him about the alleged confession a few minutes before the degradation, he swore on the head of his wife and children that he was innocent, that he had never confessed, that he had always defended his honor, and he fell back into his chair like an automaton, his mouth horribly twisted. "I recognized these pathetic phrases," Paléologue wrote, "having heard them on the sinister morning of the degradation: they gave me then the intimate certitude that Dreyfus was lying. Why do they sound still equally false to my ear today, when *I know* that he is telling the truth? Why is that man incapable of warmth when he speaks? Why even in his most strenuous protestations can nothing of his soul escape from his strangled throat? . . . There is something about him both incomprehensible and fatal, like a hero of ancient tragedy." At the end of Cavaignac's testimony, a powerful synthesis of the arguments of the General Staff intended to crush Dreyfus and his supporters, Paléologue was moved to pity, mixed with repugnance, by its effect on Dreyfus: "Pale, confused, mouth agape, he listens with gloomy stupefaction to the irrefutable demonstration of his guilt. Another moment and his eyes cloud over, drops of sweat appear on his temples, his entire visage expresses atrocious distress. He seems to be saying, 'Do what you want with me, I can't go on!'" Paléologue's impression was similar when the president of the tribunal, moments before the judges retired, asked Dreyfus whether he had any statement to make, and "Dreyfus, looking like a corpse, mumbles indistinctly some words: 'I am innocent . . . The honor of my name that my children bear . . . Your loyalty, your justice . . .' And he falls back on his chair. Sweat runs down his forehead."[31]

As required by the military code of justice, the accused was not in the courtroom when the sentence was pronounced by the president of the tribunal. It was read to him afterward by the clerk of the court. During that "formality, which was accomplished before an armed guard, the accused," Paléologue noted, "remained rigid and did not show the least emotion."[32] A few hours later, Paléologue took the train for Paris. The monstrous trial was over.

It had been a beautiful August and early September. On two Sundays, Paléologue had been called to Paris for consultations with his minister. When not busy with professional duties, he arranged to take his rest away from Rennes and as pleasantly as possible. He went to Saint-Malo and Dinard, where he lunched with an elegant anti-Dreyfusard friend and tried to explain to him the "disconcerting psychology of the accused." Afterward he walked on the rocky shore and tried to think about nothing. Suffering, it seems, always "takes place / While someone else is eating or opening a window, or just walking dully along." Tuesday, August 15, was the Feast of the Assumption. Paléologue went for the day to Combourg and revisited the chateau to which Chateaubriand had devoted some of the most beautiful pages of his *Mémoires d'Outre-tombe.* But he found that it would have been better if he hadn't come: the odious ghosts of Rennes gave him no respite. Another very gay lunch took place in Dinard, at the beautiful villa of the prefect. The sea shimmered azure and silver under a perfect azure sky. Earlier that week, there had been an attempt to assassinate Labori, but the bullet fortunately had missed his spine and been removed without difficulty. The prefect of the region reported that his police had been unable to catch the assailant, who was being protected by the local population. The prefect regretted the time when one could have made a recalcitrant witness speak by holding his feet to the fire.[33]

After a heartrending meeting at the prison with his brother directly after the judgment had been read to him, Mathieu Dreyfus rushed to Paris and went to see Joseph Reinach, whose friendship with Prime Minister Waldeck-Rousseau made him at this time crucially important. Mathieu told Reinach that he feared for his brother's life: if Alfred remained in prison he would be dead within six months. Reinach responded that a presidential pardon was the only available solution. If granted quickly, it would not only get Dreyfus out of prison but would also be perceived as the vindication of his cause. Public opinion would take it to mean that the prime minister and the minister of war had torn up the military tribunal's iniquitous verdict. Reinach undertook to call on Waldeck-Rousseau while Mathieu consulted with Georges Clemenceau, Jaurès, and other important Dreyfusards and close friends.

There was no need to persuade either Waldeck-Rousseau or Galliffet. They had already come to the conclusion that a pardon would be necessary. However, it soon became apparent that the execution of the plan was beset by problems. The first to surface was of a legal nature. Demange had as a matter of course given notice of appeal to a military commission charged with reviewing court-martial judgments. That action had prevented the Rennes decision from becoming final, and under the law a pardon could be granted only as relief from a final judgment. The solution suggested by the socialist minister Alexandre Millerand, who was himself a Dreyfusard, was for Dreyfus to withdraw the appeal. The idea horrified Mathieu and Reinach since it could be interpreted as an acquiescence by Dreyfus in the scandalous judgment. Mathieu countered by proposing that the government instead take steps to hasten the consideration of the appeal—which he and everyone else assumed would be denied—and obtain finality of the judgment through that procedure. Millerand argued strongly against this course: he foresaw the possibility that the military review commission would overturn the court-martial sentence for an error of form and send Dreyfus before another court-martial. If that happened, the risk of another guilty verdict was high, this time without extenuating circumstances, as well as of a much harsher sentence that would include a new degradation ceremony. Although Mathieu did not know it, Waldeck-Rousseau had already sought advice from Mornard in order to explore the possibility of the government's seeking immediate review by the court of the judgment on the ground that an abuse of power had occurred: the court-martial had strayed beyond the confines of the question that the Court of Cassation had instructed it to consider. Mornard's advice, like Millerand's, was not favorable. He feared that success before the court would in all probability again result in a remand before a new court-martial that was just as likely as the one in Rennes to find Dreyfus guilty, with the consequences Millerand apprehended. Waldeck-Rousseau had been one of the most successful lawyers in France. He could not help agreeing with Mornard's analysis.

Mathieu obviously could not commit his brother to withdrawing the appeal to the military commission. Moreover, given the symbolic meaning of that step, he was not willing to persuade him to take it without the concurrence of those whose role in the struggle had been of the greatest importance: with Zola absent in England, these included Reinach, Jaurès, and Clemenceau. Reinach was prepared to recommend that the appeal be withdrawn. The further discussions were not without bitterness. Clemenceau held that a presidential pardon would make it impossible to continue the struggle for Dreyfus's full vindication. If all that happened was that Dreyfus was released from prison, the country would be deprived of the moral benefit of the huge effort that had been made on his behalf. In the end, however, both Jaurès and Clemenceau agreed with the decision to withdraw the military appeal and seek a pardon. Clemenceau's grudging comment was that if he were Dreyfus's brother he too would accept the presidential grace. Somewhat later he would observe that it was very well for Dreyfus to look out for Dreyfus. As for himself and other Dreyfusards like him, their thoughts were all for their country.

Jaurès drew up the statement that Dreyfus would make in order to preserve as far as possible his dignity and proclaim that he was not giving up the struggle to clear his name: "The government of the republic gives me back my freedom. It means nothing to me without my honor. Starting today, I will continue to pursue the repair of the frightful judicial error of which I am still the victim. I want all of France to know, after a definitive judgment, that I am innocent. My heart will know no rest until not one Frenchman is left who holds me responsible for a crime that was committed by someone else."[34]

Dreyfus was too ill, too eager to be reunited with his wife and children, to refuse to follow his brother's advice. He authorized the abandonment of the appeal. This action, although backed unanimously by his principal supporters and advisers (reluctantly in the case of Clemenceau), exposed the fault lines along which bonds of friendships and allegiances forged by Dreyfusards would soon be riven. On one side would remain Clemenceau, Labori, and soon Picquart. Charles Péguy, the poet and an early Dreyfusard who had been drawn to the movement by his friend Lazare, put their position this way: "But what is most tragic, is precisely that [Dreyfus] doesn't have the right to be a private person. The fact is that we have constantly the right to call him to account, the right and *the duty* to call him to account with the utmost severity. With the utmost rigor."[35]

As we have seen Péguy never forgave what he perceived as the Dreyfus family's shabby treatment of Lazare once Alfred's freedom had been won, including Alfred's later failure to attend Lazare's funeral, even though his absence had been justified by legitimate concerns about his own safety and that of others. "He did not die for himself; but several others have died for him . . . ," Péguy wrote; "he did not ruin himself in his own cause. He will not ruin himself for anyone else. But many others have ruined themselves for him. Many have sacrificed for him their careers, their bread, even their lives, the bread of their wives and of their children."[36] One of those who sacrificed himself, according to Péguy, was Lazare, who had found that his identification as a leading advocate for Dreyfus had made it extremely difficult for him to obtain journalistic assignments.

But Péguy was far too lucid to stop there, and he was able to encapsulate the paradox of a man who did not seek martyrdom being accused by his adherents of not continuing his career as a martyr: "Dreyfus returned and almost immediately, during the first steps that were taken, during the first conversations, at the first contact, everyone suddenly had the impression that something was wrong, that it wasn't quite it, that he was such as he was and not such as we had dreamed. Some were already complaining. Some accused him at first quietly and soon publicly.

Quietly, publicly, Bernard Lazare defended him . . . 'I don't know what they want,' he would say, laughing and not laughing, laughing on the outside but not inside; 'I don't know what they are asking. I don't know what they want from him.' *Because he was unjustly condemned,* one asks of him everything, *he should have all the virtues.* **He is innocent; that is already a lot.**"[37]

On the other side of the ideological divide would remain steadfastly Mathieu Dreyfus, who wanted above all to save his brother and restore him to a normal and eventually happy family life; Jaurès; Reinach; Trarieux; and, until their premature deaths, Lazare himself and above all Zola. For all their engagement in politics, the latter three did not withhold their friendship or affection from the victim they had done so much to save. As for Dreyfus, he had emerged from the Rennes trial broken. Paléologue had thought he had looked like a corpse. The decision to do what was required in order to secure the pardon had been made by Dreyfus in extremis. He remained passionately committed to clearing his name and at the same time stolidly uninterested in making what remained of his case into a political struggle against militarism and the power of the army or for social justice.

As it turned out, the hope for an immediate, or even a rapid, grant of pardon, one that would have been tantamount to the civilian government's indignant rejection of the iniquitous military verdict, proved to be a chimera. The day before the Rennes verdict, General de Galliffet had written to Waldeck-Rousseau warning the prime minister against pitting the army and the majority of the French population against his cabinet, Dreyfusards, and Dreyfus's vociferous supporters abroad. In fact, it was difficult to find an anti-Dreyfusard outside France, and passions throughout the civilized world were running high. As soon as the Rennes verdict became known there were calls in the press for a boycott of the Universal Exhibition scheduled to open in Paris in 1900; anti-French demonstrations broke out in New York, London, Milan, and Naples; French embassies needed police protection against mob violence. But the habitual prudence of Emile Loubet, the president of the republic, and his unwillingness to take any risk had been exacerbated by his unpopularity and the attacks in the press linking him to the Panama Canal scandal. He refused to take an action that would be interpreted as a slap in the face of the army. The price of obtaining his agreement to grant the pardon turned out to be presenting it as a humanitarian gesture required by the state of Dreyfus's health.

A physician was sent to examine Dreyfus in the Rennes prison and reported that the prisoner was a "finished man." This made it possible for General de Galliffet to propose that the president issue a decree that referred to Dreyfus's alarming condition and to characterize the pardon as *un acte de haute humanité* (action of lofty humanity). Loubet signed the pardon on September 19; by bitter coincidence Auguste Scheurer-Kestner died the same morning. In order to avoid hostile crowds, it was necessary for Dreyfus to leave the prison in the middle of the night. Traveling by train and carriage under police protection, Alfred and Mathieu reached their sister and brother-in-law's property near Carpentras a day later. Alfred's wife joined him there that evening, and the children were brought the next day by Lucie's parents.

Two days after the grant of the pardon, on September 21, Galliffet issued a general order to the army that was read aloud at the company, battery, and squadron level. It proclaimed: "The incident is closed. The military judges, surrounded by the respect of all, have rendered their verdict with complete independence. Without any reservation, we bow to their decision. We also bow to the sentiment of profound pity that has guided the president of the republic."[38] The order infuriated Dreyfusard opinion; Waldeck-Rousseau, the prime minister, feeling he had been stabbed in the back, refused to have it published in the *Journal officiel* of the republic. But that was all. He did not ask for his minister's resignation. Galliffet wanted to save the face of the army, and both he and Waldeck-Rousseau wanted to calm the country. The search for justice had to take a back seat to the latter goal, which was their primary concern.

In an article titled "Le Cinquième Acte," published in *L'Aurore* three days after the guilty verdict in Rennes, Zola wrote:

> We had imagined that the trial in Rennes was the fifth act of the terrible tragedy through which we have been living for nearly two years. . . . But we were mistaken. We are faced with a new ambush, the most unexpected, the most atrocious of all, darkening the drama even more and thrusting it toward an unknown ending, before which our reason falters and fails.
>
> The Rennes trial was decidedly only the fourth act. . . . What then will be the fifth? Of what new pain and suffering will it consist, and into what supreme expiation will it plunge the nation? For it is certain that an innocent man cannot be convicted twice and that, if such were the denouement it would make the sun turn dark, and the peoples of the world would rebel![39]

The cathartic fifth act began in 1903, after considerable political changes had taken place in France. But before it could commence, there was time for another shameful, albeit perhaps necessary, entr'acte. On November 19, 1899, Waldeck-Rousseau sent to the Senate his proposed amnesty law, which covered all crimes committed in connection with the Dreyfus Affair. The sole exception was the crime of which Dreyfus had been convicted by the Rennes court: Waldeck-Rousseau wished to protect Dreyfus's right to obtain complete exoneration through eventual judicial review. However, the amnesty extinguished the many still pending judicial proceedings—for instance, those against Zola and Picquart—and it protected from criminal liability the villains of the case: Mercier, Boisdeffre, Gonse, du Paty, Lauth, and Gribelin. The law was enacted in the last days of 1900 over the strenuous opposition of Dreyfus, Zola, and Picquart. Dreyfus feared that without the ability to pursue the cabal before the tribunals he would not be able to gather the evidence of "new facts" that was required in order for the Court of Cassation to consider the validity of the Rennes verdict. Picquart had by this time his own Picquart Affair to worry about: litigation over his having been discharged from the army pursuant to a military commission's ruling, which he was appealing before the Conseil d'Etat, the highest administrative tribunal in France. He withdrew it just as it seemed likely that it would succeed, and that he might even be offered a command, issuing a statement to the effect that he was not willing to accept anything from a government that had not dared to prosecute criminals in high places.

The political change resulting from the decline of the clerical and nationalist right began to be felt in 1903. Emile Combes, a determined anti-clericalist, had become prime minister; General Louis André, equally anti-clericalist and equally devoted to republican ideals, was minister of war. Jaurès, as the leader of the socialist group in the Chamber of Deputies, was also in a position of strength. In consultation with Dreyfus, Trarieux, Clemenceau, and Dreyfus's lawyers, he decided that the time had come for the Dreyfus Affair to be brought to a real conclusion—not through pardon or amnesty but once again through judicial review. In May, during a masterful speech of marathon length that rivaled in brilliance and incisiveness his *Les Preuves,* he laid out the proof of Dreyfus's innocence and analyzed the crimes committed by those who had conspired to send him to Devil's Island and keep him there. The session degenerated into a shouting match, with an exchange of violent insults between the right- and left-wing parties, but before it was over General André intervened, declaring that the government was prepared to undertake an administrative inquiry into Jaurès's charges. The debate ended with a vote of confidence of a truly sibylline nature, to the effect that the chamber was resolved not to allow the Dreyfus case to be taken outside the judicial domain. While the meaning of that admonition was mulled over, Dreyfus addressed a petition to the minister of war requesting an investigation into new facts known to him relating to his case. Faced with this additional conundrum, the prime minister authorized General André to conduct a "personal" investigation of the matter, designed to serve the cause of truth.

André appointed his aide-de-camp and the ministry's chief

lawyer to sift through the mass of files that had been assembled for the Rennes trial and then dispersed. They were also to examine documents that had not been produced because Henry, Gonse, and the chameleonlike Louis Cuignet, who, after having denounced the faux Henry, had changed into the most virulent of anti-Dreyfusards, had considered them favorable to Dreyfus. André personally went over the entire dossier. The discoveries revealed an extent of malfeasance that was greater than what had been expected. The inventory would include, in addition to the faux Henry, at least two other documents that had been modified by Henry, a fraudulent set of bookkeeping records relating to a spy whose forged reports incriminated Dreyfus and were used at the 1894 trial, and other writings designed to incriminate Picquart in the wasteful management of funds in the Statistics Section's secret espionage accounts. The investigation took about six months, and the file was finally transmitted to the minister of justice in November 1903 by order of the cabinet.

The minister could have requested on his own motion that the Court of Cassation grant a review of the Rennes judgment. The politics of the cabinet were such, however, that Dreyfus was given to understand that a petition from him, this time for judicial review, would be appropriate, based on revelations made by Jaurès, on what he believed the André investigations had found, on perjured testimony at the Rennes trial, and, in a remarkable illustration of reliance on hearsay in French judicial proceedings, on a letter from the former German ambassador to Reinach stating that Schwartzkoppen had confessed to him that the spy who had sold him French military secrets was indeed Esterhazy. After more political complications had arisen and been resolved, on Christmas Day 1903 the minister submitted the Rennes judgment to the Court of Cassation.

The excruciatingly slow proceedings before the court—impeded by the illness of one of the judges charged with preparing a final report on the case and the need to replace him—finally ended at half past six in the evening on July 11, 1906. The court voted unanimously to reverse the Rennes judgment, and 31 to 18 to do so without remand, thus excluding the possibility of sending Dreyfus to a new court-martial, a result that was possible under a provision of the law that made a new trial unnecessary if the Court of Cassation overturned the judgment in such a manner that nothing in it survived that constituted a crime or an offence. The judgment was read in public the next day at noon. The man from Devil's Island had been declared innocent, and the stain of dishonor washed away. As cables and letters of congratulation began to flood in, Dreyfus recalled those who had died before the triumph of the cause they had done so much to bring about: Lazare, Zola, Scheurer, Trarieux, and others whose names were less illustrious. He received a letter of vintage intransigence from Picquart, to whom he had written to express his gratitude. "My dear Dreyfus," Picquart wrote, "Thank you for your note. I can imagine your joy and the joy of your family. I would have preferred, as you know, a court-martial, but I am not stubborn. Perhaps it is better this way."[40]

The next day, Friday, July 13, the French legislature adopted two laws, one conferring on Dreyfus the rank of major and the other making Picquart a brigadier general. On the afternoon of

July 20 Dreyfus was decorated with the insignia of a chevalier of the Legion of Honor in the Cour Desjardins of the Ecole militaire, which, Dreyfus recalled, had not changed since the time when he was a lieutenant posted there with a battery of horse-drawn artillery. The memory of the degradation ceremony was so strong that Dreyfus felt his heart beat as though it would break, his face turned red, and sweat covered his brow.

Justice had been done, and ostensibly the state had made reparation for the judicial error and its consequences. But all was not well. The courtyard of the Ecole militaire that the government had chosen for the decoration ceremony was a small one, and the number of guests who could be invited was limited: the Dreyfus family, Picquart, Anatole France, one of the Court of Cassation judges. Neither Jaurès nor Dreyfus's lawyers nor Reinach, nor General André, could be included. In addition, the law that had made Picquart a general had taken into account the years of service he had been deprived of by the wrongful prosecution to which he had been subjected by the General Staff cabal. In the case of Dreyfus, however, pursuant to the law his time in grade as a major commenced only on the date that rank was conferred on him, and all the time he would have accrued had he not been convicted in 1894, or had he been acquitted in 1899 rather than pardoned, was disregarded. The consequence for the forty-seven-year-old major was that officers of his age who had been comrades had all become his superiors. The beautiful career he had imagined had come to a dead end. Social contacts among officers of unequal rank were discouraged in the French army. Having returned to active service with an artillery unit at the fort of

Vincennes on October 15, 1906, twelve years to the day after he was accused of treason and arrested, he came rapidly to the conclusion that his situation was untenable. He retired from the army in 1907. His bitterness knew no bounds. Since he had not served two years as a major, upon retirement his rank was reduced to that which he had held before. He was once more a captain.

In the meantime, Georges Clemenceau, in no small measure because of his role as a leading Dreyfusard, had became prime minister and had named General Picquart his minister of war. Dreyfus, who had been attempting through various means, including the intervention of friends, to correct the injustice of his having been reintegrated into the army without seniority, undertook to appeal personally to his heroic defender. Picquart received him in General Boisdeffre's old office, and the two men reminisced about the scene there when du Paty had ordered Dreyfus to write down the text of the bordereau. At some point, Picquart expressed his regret at having lent himself to that "lugubrious comedy." But, when Dreyfus explained the purpose of his visit, the general became glacial and told him that the error, if it were one, should have been corrected by the previous government. Dreyfus understood that it was time to take his leave and did so, congratulating Picquart on his cabinet position. Picquart remarked that it was thanks to Dreyfus that he had obtained it, to which Dreyfus replied, "No, it is because you have done your duty."[41]

Dreyfus died at his home on July 12, 1935, exactly twenty-nine years after the public reading of the judgment of the Court of Cassation that had exonerated him. He had returned to active service upon the outbreak of World War I, serving first in the military northern zone of Paris and then at the front, with an artillery command based in close proximity to Verdun and the Chemin des Dames. By the end of the war he had become a lieutenant colonel and had been promoted to the rank of officer of the Legion of Honor. His son Pierre had fought courageously as a young officer on the battlefields of the Somme and Verdun; he was promoted to the rank of captain in 1920 and decorated with the Legion of Honor in 1921. Mathieu Dreyfus's only son, Emile, fell in battle in 1915. His son-in-law, the husband of his only daughter and the son of Joseph Reinach, was killed in the first year of the war. Lucie Dreyfus died at her home in Paris on December 14, 1945. She had fled to the so-called Zone libre, the Vichy-controlled part of France, and spent the remaining war years hidden in a convent under the name Madame Duteil. Her granddaughters Simone and Madeleine and grandsons Jean-Louis and Etienne, children of Alfred and Lucie's only daughter, Jeanne, had all been in the Resistance. Madeleine was caught by the Gestapo and died of typhus at the Auschwitz-Birkenau camp in January 1944. Pierre's son Charles had fought in the ranks of the Free French.

In 1984 the French state commissioned the sculptor and cartoonist Tim (Louis Mittelberg) to execute a sculpture of Dreyfus. It portrays an officer standing at attention, in his hand a broken sword. Finding a suitable site for the sculpture proved difficult. Permission to place it in the courtyard of the Ecole militaire, the scene of the degradation, was denied, as was the proposal to place it at the Ecole polytechnique, where Dreyfus had been a student. The statue finally found a temporary home in the park of the Tuileries. In 1994 it was moved to the tiny place Pierre-Lafue, near the Metro station Notre-Dame-des-Champs, in the sixth arrondissement. In 2002 it was splashed from head to foot with yellow paint, and the pedestal was covered by anti-Semitic graffiti. Also in 1994, a small square at the intersection of avenue Emile Zola and rue du Théâtre in the fifteenth arrondissement was named place Alfred Dreyfus. In 1998, on the hundredth anniversary of the publication of Zola's "J'accuse," a plaque recalling Captain Dreyfus, who had been punished for a crime he had not committed, was affixed to a wall of the courtyard of the Ecole militaire in which he was degraded.

A campaign was mounted in 2006, the hundredth anniversary of the exoneration of Dreyfus, to have his remains moved to the Panthéon. The initiative was rejected on the ground that the Panthéon is a place of repose for heroes rather than victims. But on July 12, 2006, President Jacques Chirac eulogized Dreyfus at a commemoration ceremony in the Ecole militaire courtyard, stating unambiguously that Dreyfus had not committed treason. He recognized in him a patriot who loved France passionately, and a man "to whom justice has not been done completely: with death in his soul, because he had not benefited from the reconstitution of a career to which he had a right, the officer was obliged to leave the army. That is why the Nation owed it to herself to pay him today solemn homage." These were fine and courageous words to pronounce in the lion's den, the vital center of an army that has accepted only reluctantly the innocence of Dreyfus and the guilt of his superiors. In 2006 as well, the French postal service issued a commemorative stamp bearing the likeness of Dreyfus. The speech at the Ecole militaire is not the only example of President Chirac's determination to confront moments of shame in French history. It had required even greater courage to pronounce the speech of July 16, 1995, the fifty-third anniversary of the Rafle du Vel' d'Hiv, the roundup of Paris Jews, who were then assembled at the Vélodrome d'Hiver, an indoor stadium in Paris, and deported to concentration camps. In the course of the speech Chirac acknowledged the responsibility of the French state for the crimes committed against French Jews by the Vichy regime, something that no president of the republic had done before.

The great puzzle of the Dreyfus Affair has nothing to do with mysteries such as the possible secret connection between Henry and Esterhazy or the theory favored by Paléologue that a ring of traitors, including Maurice Weil, a Jewish officer with a special link to General Saussier (his wife was the general's mistress), Esterhazy, and a high-ranking general he does not name, with the connivance of Henry and Lauth, had been selling secrets to the German, Austrian, and Italian general staffs. The true puzzle is why Dreyfus, having spent five years on Devil's Island and more than six years afterward in a struggle to clear his name, wanted so desperately to return to the French army. He was still rich, he was still married to a much younger woman of great nobility of mind and spirit, he had two children whom he loved, he was forty-seven, and he was broken in body. He would never fully recover his health. The contemptuous dislike of his former colleagues must have penetrated his consciousness after the Rennes trial, even if he had blocked it out during the court-martial in 1894. He had seen that against all reason five of his seven judges in Rennes had brought themselves to find him guilty, and he had observed at close quarters the perfidy of Mercier and Boisdeffre, the military chiefs he admired. But all the same he wanted to spend the rest of his active life in the company of their likes. How could that be?

The answer to the puzzle is almost surely to be found somewhere in the matter-of-fact report by Franz Kafka concerning the violent anti-Jewish riots that marked the first two years of the newly created independent Republic of Czechoslovakia and reached their climax on November 16, 1920: a mob stormed the building of the Jewish Rathaus in Prague, devastating archives and trampling on Torahs. Aghast at what he saw, Kafka wrote, "I've been spending every afternoon outside in the streets, wallowing in anti-Semitic hate. The other day I heard someone call Jews a 'mangy race.' Isn't it natural to leave a place where one is so hated? (Zionism or national feeling isn't needed for this at all.) The heroism of staying is nonetheless merely the heroism of cockroaches which cannot be exterminated, even from the bathroom."[42] Oppressed, tormented, and scorned over the course of so many centuries, emancipated Jews had fallen in love with their new freedom and with the good news that they could be like other people. It was up to them. If they worked hard, if they were good citizens, they would be able to spread their wings. The promise was beautiful, but it did not reckon with a hard fact that had probably not been obvious during those intoxicating days.

"Other people" did not want Jews to be like them. They wanted Jews out of the way. But Jews did not know how to make themselves so small that they would give no offense. Instead they clung to the place they had thought was theirs: for Dreyfus the army and his rank.

"dreyfus was rehabilitated, picquart became minister of war, and nobody said boo"

Zola would have seemed destined to write a great novel about France in the 1890s, one that held up a mirror to French society and forced it to confront the affair in all its ugliness. That is what he had done powerfully in earlier novels, such as *La Curée* and *L'Argent,* which exposed the financial scandals and political and sexual corruption under the Second Empire; *L'Assommoir,* a study of the Paris slums; and *La Débâcle,* which delved into the causes of the French defeat in 1870. He tried to deal with the affair in *Vérité,* which was published posthumously in 1903, but he made a strategic mistake: he transposed the Dreyfus case so that it became the story of a Jewish schoolteacher wrongly accused of the rape and murder of his own half-Jewish twelve-year-old hunchbacked nephew. In the process he diminished the scope of his subject. Perhaps he had found the direct approach that had served him so well in *La Débâcle* uncongenial in this case. In any event, although Zola was only sixty-two when he died, the creative force that had carried him triumphantly through the twenty novels of the Rougon-Macquart cycle had begun to wane. *Vérité* is not among his better works.

Anatole France, another great novelist and Zola's near contemporary, was also a fervent Dreyfusard. A member of the Académie française since 1896, skeptical, exquisitely cultivated, and writing in the mainstream of French classicism, France was at antipodes with Zola and his naturalist novels. But he threw himself unsparingly into the hurly-burly of Dreyfusard political meetings, and in 1902, putting aside past literary quarrels, he delivered the principal eulogy at Zola's funeral. Blum recalled that at the beginning of his own career as a Dreyfusard he would not have dared hope that France would become engaged in the cause; later he came to understand how it had happened. The reason was France's "rationalist faith." He was a Dreyfusard because his intelligence told him that Dreyfus was not guilty; it also told him that his certainty must be translated into action. At a time when the fortunes of the Dreyfusard movement were low, France gave a rousing speech at a public meeting and concluded by promising: "Nous aurons raison parce que nous avons raison," we will be proved right because we are right. The affair plays an important role in three of France's works, including the dystopian, often burlesque satire *L'Ile des Pingouins* (Penguin Island), published in book form in 1908 after serialization in the *New York Herald* in 1905–7. In the tradition that stretches from Jonathan Swift's *Gulliver's Travels* through Franz Kafka's "A Report to an Academy" and George Orwell's *Animal Farm* to Art Spiegelman's *Maus,* it narrates French history, the affair included, in the guise of an account of the past, present, and future of a colony of penguins. France's two other novels in which the Dreyfus Affair is like the eight-hundred-pound gorilla whose presence cannot be ignored are *L'Anneau d'améthyste* (The Amethyst Ring) and *Monsieur Bergeret à Paris* (Monsieur Bergeret in Paris), which form volumes 3 and 4 of his *Histoire contemporaine,* a cycle of four novels. Both were written while the affair was still unfolding, before Dreyfus's exoneration; they are eyewitness reports.[1]

By far the greatest work of fiction that takes the affair as a major theme is Marcel Proust's *A la recherche du temps perdu.* Thirty-one years younger than Zola, and twenty-seven years younger than France, Proust became convinced of Dreyfus's innocence early, as did his younger brother, Dr. Robert Proust. Marcel was one of the brilliant young men whom Blum used to see at the editorial offices of *Banquet,* an avant-garde literary monthly Proust co-founded, for which both Blum and he wrote. They also met at the Dreyfusard salon of Madame Emile Straus, the widow of the composer Georges Bizet and current wife of a leading business lawyer whose clients included the Rothschilds. As happened in many families, Marcel and Robert's father, Dr. Adrien Proust, a high civil servant, was opposed to judicial review of the 1894 court-martial sentence and for a time refused to speak to his Dreyfusard sons. The family quarrel was not long lasting; Dr. Proust came around to accepting the necessity of review.

Proust was also the author of *Jean Santeuil,* an unfinished and intensely autobiographical *Bildungsroman* begun in 1895, when he was twenty-three, and abandoned in the early 1900s, before Dreyfus's exoneration; it was not published until after Proust's death in 1922. *Jean Santeuil* relates the debut in society, and the friendships and first loves, of an intellectual, sensitive young Parisian bourgeois. As might be expected, he is riveted by the Zola libel trial. The importance of *Jean Santeuil,* apart from its standing as Proust's first attempt to develop the great themes of *A la recherche* in the context of a novel, lies in its depiction of the feverish excitement that surrounded the Zola trial. Young men head early in the morning for the Palais de Justice, the courthouse on the Ile de la Cité, as though to a corrida, and they handicap the contestants, the witnesses, and their lawyers. They bring sandwiches and thermoses of coffee to be consumed in the courtroom in the seats they are fortunate to have secured and do not dare leave for fear that someone will take them. Often entrance to the courtroom can be obtained only through a well-placed lawyer friend.

The most striking passage in the novel is the poetic portrait of General de Boisdeffre. There is no better or subtler illustration of the prevalent French cult of the army. Without that cult, and the concomitant fear of the trauma of laying bare the mediocre criminality of a minister of war—perhaps two ministers, if one counts General Billot as well as Mercier—and the chief of the General Staff, the Dreyfus Affair would not have been possible.

We have seen the way Boisdeffre threw down the gauntlet to members of the jury in the Zola trial, telling them that they must choose between trusting the military chiefs, whose duty was to defend the nation, and the risk that the chiefs would leave that thankless and arduous task to others if they were rejected. Proust's portrait shows Boisdeffre on the afternoon of the day before, directly after General de Pellieux's ill-advised recitation of the faux Henry, arriving at the Palais de Justice in response to Pellieux's appeal for help. He is late: the court has adjourned, perhaps because the presiding judge deemed it prudent to give the minister of war time to instruct Boisdeffre on what he was allowed to say on the witness stand. Boisdeffre is in mufti, a hugely tall top hat on his head, advancing slowly, one leg stiff as though it had been often broken in falls from a horse. He is still young looking, but his cheeks are covered by a leprous mold of red and violet broken veins, his eyes blink, he appears calm even though he is obviously preoccupied. Jean takes in the apparition, and realizes that it is

> that august thing called "General de Boisdeffre." . . . It was with those blinking eyes that he looked around, it was the cigars he smoked and the cognac he drank after too long workdays that had gilded and reddened his cheeks. People raised their hats as he passed, and he returned the greetings with a great deal of politeness, like a man of altogether preponderant rank, a clerical grandee, who could incite to envy but wanted to disarm by being very polite. . . . So he returned the salutations but without seeming to have seen them, following his own thought, at times blinking, holding his leg stiff, halting, pulling on his moustache, passing his hand over his reddened cheeks as though over an old warhorse he had fatigued. And while he mounted the stairs, followed by his aide-de-camp, everyone asked

himself anxiously what he was going to say, and these reddened cheeks, these blinking eyes, and even the half-opened overcoat and the enormous top hat askew on his head, these banal things were contemplated with an irresistible emotion by all those who would not have dared to approach without respect, a feeling that they were charged with an unheard-of, immense, European force . . . which was going to explode suddenly and change, with the life of one man and one family, the lot of Europe.[2]

Shortly after the visit to the Palais de Justice (and therefore after the guilty verdict in the Zola trial and while Picquart is confined in the Mont-Valérien fortress), Jean attends an elegant dinner and hears a distinguished general who had been a minister of war express with great authority his view of the affair. He declares that although he does not believe that Dreyfus is guilty, he is certain that Esterhazy is innocent; that the bordereau was not written by Esterhazy, but his handwriting had been imitated; that the guilty party is someone well known whose name for the time being he cannot reveal; and that Picquart forged the petit bleu because he believed equally firmly that Esterhazy was guilty and that Dreyfus was innocent, his forgery thus having been designed to bring into the open the relations between Esterhazy and Schwartzkoppen, of the existence of which Picquart had become certain. While the other guests listen in rapt silence, Jean notices that his hostess is looking at her husband out of the corner of her eye as though to say, "All the same we have quite a salon, and what choice dishes we put before our guests!"[3]

Proust took evident pleasure in placing such dishes before the reader. *A la recherche* has more than enough material in it for a *sottisier* of the affair, a commonplace book of inanities that

Flaubert would have surely wanted to include in *Bouvard et Pé-cuchet* if he had lived long enough to see the French follies of the 1890s, with their intertwined mantras of nationalism and anti-Semitism. Above all, however, the affair was for Proust a catalyst for social change, making possible alliances that would otherwise have seemed unnatural, lifting some to surprising social heights and provoking the ostracism of others. The impact of the affair on French society is one more illustration of Proust's vast concept of the power of time to transform the perception of persons and places. It serves as well as a metaphor for a phenomenon that Proust did not confront directly: the rise of new industrial and financial fortunes and the displacement by the new bourgeoisie of the old French aristocracy, whose diminishing wealth and willful refusal to concern themselves with the affairs of the despised republic relegates them to the status of self-deluded fops.

The pervasive anti-Semitism of arriviste converted Jews, a major theme in France's *L'Anneau d'améthyste* and *M. Beregeret à Paris,* is strikingly absent from *A la recherche.* The sole, lacerating example in Proust's novel is the behavior of Charles Swann's daughter Gilberte. Swann, who competes with the Narrator and the emblematic homosexual Baron de Charlus for the status of most important character in the work, is a Catholic Jew (he was either baptized at birth or converted later) who has the most eminent social position of any Jew in France. He is at home and at ease in the faubourg Saint-Germain; among his friends are princes of the blood; he is the pet and favored companion of the Duchess de Guermantes, a redoubtable epitome of aristocratic chic and hauteur. To the horror of his friends, Swann marries a former cocotte, Odette de Crécy. Sold by her mother as a twelve-year-old to a roué, Odette has made her way through the various stages in which a prostituted child ascends to the status of a demi-mondaine, kept by a succession of progressively richer men. The marriage with Swann follows the birth of their daughter Gilberte. After Swann's death, when Odette has become a rich woman, she marries again, this time the Count de Forcheville, a minor and impecunious aristocrat whose one merit is that he is not a Jew, with whom she had a sporadic liaison both before and during her marriage to Swann. Forcheville adopts Gilberte and gives her his name; being able to call herself Mademoiselle de Forcheville becomes useful to Gilberte in the 1890s, when anti-Semitism has become a far more potent force than previously, and her money makes almost everyone forget the obscurity of the Forcheville connection. In a shameful scene Gilberte pretends not to be acquainted with Lady Rufus Israël (her father's aunt and the wife of a prodigiously wealthy Jewish financier), who has always called Gilberte by her first name. Apropos of that piece of cowardice, the Narrator tells us that when another girl, whether maliciously or in a moment of tactlessness, asked Gilberte the name of her real father, Gilberte pronounced it "Svann," instead of the accepted "Souann." Moments later, having realized that she had made things worse by Germanizing her English name, she added lamely that there were differing accounts of her birth, insinuating that she might be the illegitimate child of a great personage. The Narrator notes that she spoke to him of Swann rarely, although he had known both Swann and her well since she was a little girl; otherwise "one didn't dare any more to pronounce the name Swann in her presence." Gilberte's lack of self-respect echoes an anecdote that the Narrator told earlier: more than one anti-Semite in French high society who counted Swann among his cherished friends found comfort in the rumor that Swann was the natural son of a royal prince, the Duke de Berry, and even pointed to a family resemblance between them.[4]

Proust may have felt that he was personally exposed when it came to the subject of Jews preferring to sweep their Jewishness under the carpet—or, indeed, to that of Jewish anti-Semitism—and had no desire to develop it further. Proust's mother's family were rich Jewish stockbrokers and manufacturers from Alsace, and his father was a Catholic provincial who had risen in the world through brilliance and hard work, with some help from his wife's money. Like Swann, Proust was on friendly terms with a dizzying array of aristocrats, ranging from nobles who were purely French to more exotic specimens, like the Romanian princes, the brothers Bibesco, and Princess Souzo, a Romanian princess who was, like her husband, Paul Morand, a notorious anti-Semite. The subject may have been too hot to handle, especially given the scathing portrayals of Jews in *A la recherche.* However, while he considered himself a Catholic Frenchman, Proust never hid his Jewish ancestry and like his brother and father was on terms of tender intimacy with his mother's family. It is also a fact that Proust was uncompromisingly courageous in his treatment of a subject that could well have been even more difficult: his own sexual orientation.

Being a homosexual did not stop Proust from making homo-sexuality in men and women one of the centerpieces of his work or from treating it as an illness and a curse. The reason for Proust's lack of interest in Jewish converts—a favorite target of France's—however, may have been the circumstance that in France baptism was not a prerequisite for ascension by an assimilated Jew to the top rung of the ladder in elegant society, the university, the government, or high finance. The Rothschild, Fould, and Deutsch de la Meurthe families for generations had combined their role as paragons of fashion with financial and industrial dominance, while the Rothschilds at the same time played a leading role in the French Jewish community; Léon Blum, Pierre Mendès-France, and Laurent Fabius all became prime minister; and the Reinach brothers had achieved eminence in French university life at the very time the Dreyfus Affair was envenoming society. (The Reinachs' success has since been replicated innumerable times across the spectrum of academic disciplines by such scholars as the anthropologist Claude Lévi-Strauss, the political scientist Raymond Aron, and François Jacob and André Lwoff, co-winners of a Nobel Prize for Physiology or Medicine.) A remarkable conversion to Protestantism was that of the distinguished Halévy family, descended from a famous rabbi. A descendant of the rabbi, Daniel Halévy, who had been an early Dreyfusard and was later a noted sociologist and cultural critic, acquired in his middle age right-wing convictions that led him to collaborate with the Vichy regime. Anatole France had died long before, but his satire of anti-Semitic Jews may have been a way of lambasting Arthur Meyer, an important political journalist and France's contemporary. Grandson of a rabbi, he had converted to Catholicism and became a fervent royalist, anti-Semite, and anti-Dreyfusard.

The first mention of the Dreyfus Affair in *A la recherche* comes in the second volume, *A l'ombre des jeunes filles en fleur* (In the Shadow of Young Girls in Flower). Society, Proust tells us, is a kaleidoscope. We are in 1895, and the kaleidoscope has turned. Those who look through it see that even the most elegant Jews have been abruptly displaced to the bottom of the field of vision, while salons and people who would have been thought ridiculous and undesirable only a short time ago have ascended. For instance, the salon of an ultra-Catholic Austrian prince has become the most brilliant in Paris, although neither politics nor bigotry had been a ticket of admission to high society since the time of Charles X, who lost his throne in the July 1830 revolution. Indeed, an elegant hostess did not invite or receive in her salon republican politicians, otherwise known as "opportunists"— the name given without any pejorative inference to politicians belonging to the group that had governed France from 1879 to 1885 and from 1890 to 1895. On the other hand, it was not unusual for a society woman to encounter in a salon a Jew as elegant as Proust's Lady Israël. Certain Jews were powerful in society, as well as finance, and none more so than Sir Rufus Israël, a man of approximately the same standing as the Rothschilds. Lady Israël's connections in faubourg Saint-Germain society were not as deeply rooted or ultra-elegant as those of her nephew Swann, but they were elegant enough for her to make certain that none of her friends received Swann's wife, Odette. (Lady Israël had deplored the marriage.) The one exception was Countess de Marsantes, sister of the Duke de Guermantes, the grandest of noblemen, who had secretly disregarded the ban but lived in fear of being found out by Lady Israël. Once the wave of anti-Dreyfusism and anti-Semitism had swept high society, however, the situations were reversed: Odette became sought after because of her nationalist and anti-Dreyfusard views, her own stylishness and charm, and Swann's wealth, while Lady Israël had turned into a pariah. So it happened in the new social order that when Odette found herself in Madame de Marsantes's salon at the same time as Lady Israël, Madame de Marsantes was careful not to introduce them. She was not apprehensive about the thunderbolt that Lady Israël might hurl at her. Far from it, she wished to spare Odette the shock of finding herself in the same room as a Jew.

Odette's trajectory mirrors the changing of the guard in French society. At the time, most upper-class Parisian women designated a day of the week on which they were at home to receive ladies of their acquaintance as well as gentlemen; custom did not, however, require the husband to accompany the wife or vice versa. Having an elegant salon, being able to draw to it people of fashion or sufficient distinction for the hostess to consider them trophies and magnets capable of attracting other luminaries, as well as society people, was a normal ambition. The result of Odette's ambiguous social position—a former cocotte married to a Jew—was that she could not attract guests from among Swann's most elegant friends. She was obliged to find them among people who were themselves excluded from the faubourg Saint-Germain and yet had some cachet. That had limited her to subcabinet-level high civil servants and their wives, a class snubbed by anti-republican aristocracy. Odette had no illusions about the reach of the Dreyfus Affair and its effect on her standing in society and rightly feared that Swann's being a Jew and an outspoken Dreyfusard would be fatal to her social ambitions and jeopardize whatever she had been able to achieve so far. Nothing could be done about Swann's ancestry, but she prevailed on him not to proclaim Dreyfus's innocence in her salon. Moreover, when he was not present, she did not scruple to voice ardent nationalist opinions. She was soon rewarded by being able to join several anti-Semitic leagues that society women were forming. Through them she was finally able to attain the goal that had seemed so hopelessly out of her reach, establishing relations with women who were pillars of the faubourg Saint-Germain aristocracy. Word had spread that she was a reliable nationalist, an anti-Semite, and "une excellente femme."

Anti-Semitism, in fact, emerges as a social grace. A great German aristocrat, rich and exceedingly well born, Prince von Faffenheim-Munsterburg-Weinigen, referred to in society as Prince Von, is seen for the first time at the "day" of the Marquise de Villeparisis, a grande dame closely related to the Guermantes. One of her nieces notes that the German nobleman is "right-thinking." By that she means that he is not a Dreyfusard like all foreigners; what is more, she adds, he is "anti-Semitism personified." Madame Swann appears at the same reception. Her presence, which would have been unimaginable a short time earlier, is no longer surprising. But the Open Sesame of anti-Dreyfusism and anti-Semitism does not always work. Madame de Villeparisis's nephew and the Narrator's best friend says to the Narrator: "I don't want my mother [Madame de Marsantes] to present me to Mme Swann. . . . She's an old tart. Her husband is Jewish and she puts on a nationalist act."[5] Sometimes a turn of the kaleidoscope is responsible for the elevation of a Jew. The Narrator is startled to see a notoriously anti-Semitic lady return with the utmost amiability the greeting of the father of one of his friends whom she knows to be Jewish. The secret reason is that they are joined by adherence to the same cause: she too believes in Dreyfus's innocence. As for the Jewish gentleman, he has come to value the anti-Semitic lady's hatred of Jews. It is such a contradiction to her belief in Dreyfus's innocence that it can be taken as a guaranty that her Dreyfusism is sincere.

Momentous changes of allegiance are part of the upheaval. When the Narrator meets Swann at a large reception given by Prince de Guermantes, he asks him why all the Guermantes are anti-Dreyfusards. Swann replies that it is because they are all anti-Semites and tells him two anecdotes about their host, a cousin of the duke, married to a Bavarian royal princess. According to Swann, the prince is so anti-Semitic that he let a wing of his chateau burn to the ground rather than borrow fire-fighting equipment from the neighboring chateau, which belonged to a Rothschild, and chose to continue to suffer from a dreadful toothache because the only dentist in the region was Jewish.

At the same reception, a rumor had begun to spread that the prince had asked to speak privately to Swann in order to show him the door. They do disappear together momentarily, but when Swann reemerges, and the incurably nosy Narrator asks whether he had been asked to leave, Swann replies, not at all. First the prince told him that he had been avoiding him in order to escape hearing Swann's opinions about the Dreyfus Affair; his and the princess's sensitivity on this subject was so great that she had scolded her brother-in-law, the Grand Duke of Hesse, for suggesting that Dreyfus was innocent. However, a year and a half earlier, in a conversation with a senior general, the prince was told that grave illegalities had occurred in the conduct of the court-martial, information that had disturbed him profoundly because of his veneration of the army. But further conversations with the general, and subsequent reading of texts that until then he had refused to look at, had left him without a doubt that such had been the case. He had said nothing to the princess about it, wanting to spare her feelings. Subsequently, the general informed him that while there had been illegalities, and the handwriting on the bordereau was perhaps not Dreyfus's, glaring proof of his guilt did exist. This was the faux Henry, and only a few days later the forgery became known. The prince had begun to read *Le Siècle,* a Dreyfusard paper, and to have his confessor—who also believed in Dreyfus's innocence—say masses for Dreyfus, his wife, and his children. Soon came a surprise as startling as any of the others: the priest revealed that the princess was also asking him to say masses for Dreyfus. She had come to believe that Dreyfus was innocent long before the prince.

An equally startling conversion was that of Duke de Guermantes, only it was farcical, in keeping with the duke's character. The vehemently anti-Dreyfusard duke traveled to a spa to take the waters and met there three charming and well-born Italian ladies who took to inviting him to be the fourth at bridge. On one occasion the conversation turned to the Dreyfus case, at which the duke declared that the captain was guilty. The ladies laughed and said that there was no proof whatsoever against him. The duke had by then formed a high opinion of their intelligence, and after a few stumbles he repeated after them, Of course he is innocent, there is no proof of his guilt to be found. Upon his return he kept repeating the lesson learned from the elegant Italians and shocked his friends by his new view of the case.

A hostess's salon and social standing could also rise by reason of her Dreyfusism. This is what happens to Madame Verdurin, the *fée Carabosse* of *A la recherche.* Colossally rich, ugly, and malevolent but possessed of a rare gift for finding and appreciating what was best in new music and art, she had built her salon around her own powerful personality and a band of faithful guests, *le petit clan,* that included at various times a painter of genius, a sculptor, an academician, a rich and very aristocratic Russian princess in disgrace with her family and other Russians, a professor of medicine whose rising reputation was matched by his vulgarity, and a great violinist. (It was there that Swann had met Odette.) Afflicted by an inferiority complex and the suspiciousness that often accompanies it, Madame Verdurin had formerly claimed that she excluded from her salon bores (*les ennuyeux*), a category that included all persons of fashion who she thought would reject her. Like Odette on account of Swann, she had begun to fear that her Dreyfusist ideas would prevent her salon from acquiring greater luster, but as it turned out it was precisely those convictions that enabled her to draw into her orbit writers of great talent who would in the future become invaluable assets for her as a hostess. Political passions waxed and waned but when, in the years following Dreyfus's rehabilitation, the affair no longer divided society, Anatole France's position as a writer of genius continued to be as lofty as before, and his value as a trophy guest was undiminished. He remained faithful to Madame Verdurin and could be found in regular attendance at her salon as well as in her loge at the theater. She had also been on Zola's side during his libel trial. In the evening Labori and Picquart had often plotted the next day's strategy in a corner of her salon, and the faithful were able to see them up close. They flocked to her house to get the most recent news. These were trophy acquisitions, and they were laying the foundation of a salon that would become all powerful during World War I, by which time Madame Verdurin had become ferociously nationalistic and anti-German.

As we have seen, the exoneration of Dreyfus in 1906 hardly caused a ripple in French society. The Narrator remarked laconically: "Dreyfus was rehabilitated, Picquart became minister of war, and nobody said boo." Other concerns were to convulse France in the next eight years, foremost among them anti-clerical reforms, social strife, and the growing international tensions that plunged Europe into World War I. The Narrator noted that as the war ground on, and afterward, pundits would throw in the cliché "in that prehistorical time" whenever they mentioned the affair.

The affair had lost its toxicity because it had been forgotten: "Dreyfusism had become integrated in a series of things both respectable and habitual. As to asking oneself about its value, no one thought of it now, no more in order to agree with it than as in the past to condemn it. It was no longer *shocking*. That was all that was required. One hardly remembered that it had been shocking, any more than one knows after a certain time whether the father of a young woman was a thief or not. If necessary, one can say: 'No, you're speaking of the brother-in-law or someone of the same name.'"[6]

By September 11, 2008, America's open-ended, apparently limitless global war on terror had been in progress for seven years. It has not been the theme of any great fiction. The likely reason is that it is not yet possible to tell the nature of the damage done to the fabric of American society by the crimes and abuses of the Bush administration committed in the course of its pursuit of the war on terror, which dwarf those of which the French army's General Staff became guilty in its implacable persecution of Captain Alfred Dreyfus. When Proust commented that one hardly remembered that the Dreyfus Affair had been "shocking," the paroxysm that had convulsed French society before Dreyfus's exoneration had long been over. Will some day in the near future the crimes of the Bush administration, like the Palmer raids of 1919 and 1920, the massive violations of the constitutional rights of Japanese Americans during World War II, and, in France, the crimes against Dreyfus, disappear under the scar tissue of silence and indifference? It is too soon to tell. The great plays and novels that will open our eyes to the work accomplished by time and its great partner oblivion remain to be written.

cast of characters

BLUM, LÉON (1872–1950) A journalist, civil servant, and socialist leader, Blum was a member of the Parisian intellectual elite. He was prime minister of France three times: in 1936–37 as the leader of the Front populaire government; for one month in 1938; and from December 16, 1946, to January 22, 1947. An early and committed Dreyfusard, Blum set down in 1935, directly after Dreyfus's death, his recollections of the affair in a series of articles published by the weekly *Marianne;* they were subsequently published as *Souvenirs sur l'Affaire.*

BOISDEFFRE, CHARLES LE MOUTON DE (1839–1919) Boisdeffre became chief of staff of the French army in 1893. A devout product of Jesuit education, he covered up and connived in the illegal machinations of the minister of war, General Auguste Mercier, under whom he served, and later of his subordinates, General Arthur Gonse and Major Joseph Henry, and their colleagues. His testimony weighed heavily in the conviction of Emile Zola in his first criminal libel trial and in that of Dreyfus by the Rennes court-martial in 1899. He retired from the army after Henry's suicide.

BRISSON, HENRI (1835–1912) Brisson was prime minister when the government finally accepted in September 1898 Lucie Dreyfus's petition for review by the Court of Cassation of the judgment of the Paris court-martial that in December 1894 had convicted Captain Alfred Dreyfus of treason.

CAVAIGNAC, GODEFROY (1853–1905) As minister of war in the government headed by Henri Brisson, Cavaignac revealed in an 1898 speech to the Chamber of Deputies the crucial documents in the dossier secret, including the faux Henry, that he thought proved Dreyfus's guilt. Shortly afterward Cavaignac's own military attaché discovered that the faux Henry was a forgery. Cavaignac resigned after Henry's suicide rather than agree to the government's petitioning for review of the Paris court-martial conviction, and for the rest of his life he remained a vocal anti-Dreyfusard.

CLEMENCEAU, GEORGES (1841–1929) Clemenceau served sporadically as a deputy to the National Assembly, until 1893, when he lost his seat as a result of an unfounded accusation that he was in the pay of Great Britain and marginal implication in the Panama Canal scandal. As editor of *L'Aurore,* Clemenceau campaigned energetically from 1897 to 1899 for judicial review of Dreyfus's conviction, publishing (and titling) Zola's open letter to President Faure, "J'accuse." Elected to the Senate in 1902, he was prime minister from 1906 to 1909 and brought Georges Picquart, by then a brigadier general, into his cabinet as minister of war. He became prime minister again in November 1917, presiding over a coalition cabinet in which he served also as his own minister of war. His implacable conduct of the war, in tandem with Marshal Ferdinand Foch, earned him the sobriquet *Père de la Victoire,* Father of the Victory. Another sobriquet, *le tigre* (Tiger), dating back to the 1880s, encapsulated his ferocity as a politician.

DEMANGE, EDGAR (1841–1925) Dreyfus's lawyer, friend, and trusted counselor, Demange defended Dreyfus in the Paris and Rennes courts-martial.

DREYFUS, LUCIE (1869–1945) Daughter of David Hadamard, a wealthy diamond dealer, and his wife, Louise, Lucie married Alfred Dreyfus on April 21, 1890. They had two children: Pierre, born in April 1891, and Jeanne, born in February 1893. Throughout the affair, Lucie campaigned strenuously for Alfred's release.

DREYFUS, MATHIEU (1857–1930) Mathieu Dreyfus, Alfred's brother, left the management of the Dreyfus family business to his two older brothers in order to devote himself full time to securing his younger brother's freedom and exoneration. After that goal had been achieved, he resumed his business career. He set down his recollections of the affair in *L'Affaire telle que je l'ai vécue* (The Affair As I Lived It).

ESTERHAZY, FERDINAND WALSIN- (1847–1923) Descendant of an illegitimate French branch of the noble and distinguished Hungarian family, Esterhazy joined the French Foreign Legion in 1870 and took part in the Franco-Prussian War. A swindler and incorrigible liar and intriguer who did not lack shrewdness or brains, he was posted to the Statistics Section in 1877, but his service there was of short duration. In July 1894, by which time he had become a major, he began his career as spy for Maximilian von Schwartzkoppen, the military attaché at the German Embassy in Paris. He was tried by court-martial in January 1897, after Mathieu Dreyfus had denounced him as the real author of the bordereau, and was acquitted. Cashiered from the army after Henry's suicide in August 1898, he fled to England and finished his life in Harpenden, in Hertfordshire, calling himself Count Jean de Volmont. In 1898 he published his twisted, often entertaining version of the affair as *Les Dessous de l'Affaire Dreyfus* (The Hidden Story of the Dreyfus Affair).

FAURE, FÉLIX (1841–1899) The president of France from January 1895 until his death in 1899, Faure revealed to Dr. Joseph Gibert that the Paris court-martial had convicted Dreyfus on the basis of the dossier secret. He thus played an important role in Dreyfus's eventual exoneration, but he remained an implacable opponent of judicial review of the 1894 court-martial.

FRANCE, ANATOLE (1844–1924) Born Jacques Anatole Thibault, France was the son of a Paris book dealer. His output as a writer was vast, and although he wrote in many genres, he is chiefly known as a novelist in the mainstream of French classicism. His first great success was *Le Crime de Sylvestre Bonnard;* in his lifetime, his most famous novel was *La Rôtisserie de la Reine Pédauque* (At the Sign of the Reine Pédauque). Having become convinced of Dreyfus's innocence, he immersed himself in the struggle for judicial review of the Paris court-martial. Three of his novels—*L'Ile des Pingouins* (Penguin Island), *L'Anneau d'améthyste* (The Amethyst Ring), and *M. Bergeret à Paris* (M. Bergeret in Paris)—concern themselves with the affair. In 1921 he received the Nobel Prize for Literature.

GONSE, CHARLES-ARTHUR (1838–1917) A French army general, Gonse was the deputy chief of staff at the time of the affair, and the head of the Statistics Section reported to him. Like General de Boisdeffre, he refused to seek the review by the Court of Cassation of the Paris court-martial; instead he directed the campaign to neutralize Picquart and exclude him from the army, and covered up or instigated Henry's criminal illegal activities. He was forced out of the army after Henry's suicide.

HENRY, JOSEPH (1846–1898) A farmer's son with rudimentary education married to an innkeeper's daughter, Henry rose in the army through the ranks and served as aide-de-camp to General de Miribel, under whose auspices he was assigned in 1877 to the Statistics Section, returning, after reassignment, in 1893, less than a year ahead of Dreyfus. Henry's role in the affair was central. It was he who perjured himself during the Paris court-martial, testifying that an intelligence source had told him that Dreyfus was the traitor at the General Staff. It was also he who forged the faux Henry and organized the campaign to force Picquart out of the army and protect Esterhazy. His suicide on August 31, 1898, made inevitable the review of the Paris court-martial's judgment and Dreyfus's eventual exoneration.

JAURÈS, JEAN (1859–1914) Like Henry a farmer's son, Jaurès was a brilliant student, winning first place in the competitive entrance examination to the prestigious Ecole normale supérieure. After passing another competitive examination, *agrégation* in philosophy, he taught philosophy first at a lycée in Albi and then at the university in Toulouse. Before long he veered toward journalism and socialist politics. Having become convinced that Dreyfus was innocent, he came to his defense in devastating articles that appeared in *La Petite République* and were later published in book form as *Les Preuves.* His masterful speech in 1903 before the Chamber of Deputies paved the way to the judicial review of the Rennes court-martial. In 1905, Jaurès became the leader of the French socialist movement. A strong believer in the universality of the socialist workers movement, he continued to argue for better relations between France and Germany and for a German workers' strike against the war. He was murdered in 1914 by a fanatical nationalist.

LAZARE, BERNARD (1865–1903) Lazare Marcus Manassé Bernard (he adopted the name of Bernard Lazare) was born into an assimilated bourgeois family that celebrated Jewish high holidays but was not otherwise religious. After studies in Paris, at the Ecole des Chartes, he veered toward anarchism and became known as an independent and astute literary critic. In the 1890s he turned toward Jewish causes and published *L'Antisémitisme, son histoire et ses causes* (1894). Mathieu Dreyfus recruited him in the spring of 1895 to help draw intellectuals to his brother's cause and soon afterward asked him to prepare a pamphlet demonstrating the illegality of the Paris court-martial's judgment. The result was *Une Erreur judiciaire: La Vérité sur l'Affaire Dreyfus* (A Judicial Error: The Truth About the Dreyfus Affair), which was distributed on November 6, 1896, to members of the Chamber of Deputies and the Senate, and to leading intellectuals. It was the first reasoned—and irrefutable—demonstration of the necessity of a judicial review of the judgment.

MERCIER DU PATY DE CLAM, ARMAND (1853–1916) Scion of an ancient family and graduate of the military academy Saint-Cyr and the Ecole d'état-major (predecessor of the Ecole supérieure de guerre), du Paty was the deputy chief of one of the bureaus of the General Staff. It was he who dictated the text of the bordereau to Dreyfus on the day he was arrested and acted as the officer in charge of the preliminary inquiry into Dreyfus's case. He was the author of the memorandum that accompanied the dossier secret delivered to the Paris court-martial judges and delivered the dossier to the president of the tribunal. Flamboyant, haughty, endowed with a wild imagination, and with a fondness for cross-dressing, du Paty was duped by Gonse and Henry into playing a major role in the plot to protect Esterhazy and ruin Picquart. He was arrested in June 1899 on charges of forgery, but they were dismissed. Having been moved into inactive reserve after Henry's suicide, he was compulsorily retired from the army in 1904. He volunteered for service at the outbreak of World War I, asking to be assigned to a front-line position, and died of wounds received in battle.

MERCIER, AUGUSTE (1833–1921) General and minister of war from December 1893 to January 1895, Mercier was the principal force behind Dreyfus's conviction at the Paris court-martial, having arranged for du Paty to deliver the dossier secret to the court-martial judges. Mercier remained an opponent of judicial review of the verdict and played an important role in securing the guilty verdict at the Rennes court-martial. He continued his persecution of Dreyfus after being elected in 1902 to the Senate and opposed the law that rehabilitated Dreyfus and reintegrated him into the army.

PALÉOLOGUE, MAURICE (1859–1944) A young, brilliant, and singularly well-connected French diplomat, Paléologue served as the Foreign Ministry liaison with the Statistics Section and as the representative of the ministry at Zola's libel trial, at the Court of Cassation's review of the Paris court-martial, and at the Rennes court-martial. His memoir of the affair, *Journal de l'Affaire Dreyfus, 1894–1899,* was published posthumously in 1955. Paléologue was a good writer, and he shaped his notes, which he took daily during the period, into a vivid narrative, but except for such editorial changes as he may have made to make himself look better, there is no reason to doubt that the journal represents his perception of the events as they unfolded. Before retiring Paléologue reached the highest rung of the French diplomatic career: the post of the secretary general of the Ministry of Foreign Affairs.

PICQUART, GEORGES (1854–1914) A model officer whose career was interrupted for almost ten years because of the stand he took in maintaining that Dreyfus was innocent, Picquart was one of the heroes of the Dreyfus case. By discovering that Esterhazy was the author of the bordereau, and that nothing in the dossier secret incriminated Dreyfus, he made Dreyfus's ultimate exoneration inevitable. Reintegrated into the army in 1906 with the rank of brigadier general, he served as Clemenceau's minister of war. After the fall of the Clemenceau cabinet he was assigned to a line command and died on January 14, 1914, from injuries suffered in a fall from his horse.

SCHEURER-KESTNER, AUGUSTE (1833–1899) A grand old man of French politics in the last two decades of the nineteenth century and a staunch defender of the republic, Scheurer had been made senator for life and was the vice president of the Senate at the time of the Dreyfus Affair. His bid for re-election failed in January 1898 as a result of the public stand he took proclaiming Dreyfus's innocence and urging judicial review of the Paris court-martial. He was principally responsible for convincing Emile Zola that Dreyfus was innocent and enlisting him in Dreyfus's cause. Scheurer died on the day Dreyfus received the presidential pardon.

SCHWARTZKOPPEN, MAXIMILIAN VON (1850–1917) The military attaché at the German Embassy in Paris from December 10, 1891, until November 11, 1897, when he was recalled to Germany to take command of a regiment of the Imperial Guard, Schwartzkoppen was the employer of Esterhazy. His carelessness with two important documents, the bordereau and the petit bleu, led to the accusation of Dreyfus of treason and to the eventual unmasking of Esterhazy. Schwartzkoppen's recollections of the affair and his role in it were written in 1903 but first published, together with an extensive commentary by his editor, in 1930. Schwartzkoppen's final military rank was that of lieutenant general of infantry (equivalent of U.S. or British major general). In 1916 he commanded an infantry division on Germany's eastern front, and died of an illness contracted in service.

ZOLA, EMILE (1840–1902) Zola shares with Mathieu Dreyfus and Picquart the credit for Dreyfus's eventual exoneration. A prodigiously gifted novelist, he is probably best known for *Thérèse Raquin,* written before the commencement of the twenty-novel Rougon-Macquart cycle, and *La Curée, L'Assommoir, Nana,* and *Germinal,* which are all part of the cycle. The publication of "J'accuse," his open letter to the president of the republic, on January 13, 1898, was a turning point of the Dreyfus Affair: it led directly to the libel case against Zola that served as a public forum in which the nullity of the charges against Dreyfus and the General Staff's illegal machinations were revealed.

chronology

1859
OCT. 9   Alfred Dreyfus is born in Mulhouse, in Alsace, at the
            time part of France. He is the youngest of the seven
            children of Raphael and Jeannette (née Libman)
            Dreyfus.
1878   Dreyfus is admitted to the Ecole polytechnique. His
            rank in the competitive entrance examination is 182nd
            out of 236 successful applicants.
1880   Dreyfus graduates from the Ecole polytechnique,
            128th out of 235, and is admitted as a second lieu-
            tenant to the Ecole d'application de l'artillerie et du
            génie, the artillery and engineering school. His rank
            in the competitive entrance examination is 38th out of
            103 successful candidates; his rank upon graduation is
            32nd out of 97.
1889   Dreyfus is promoted to the rank of captain.
1890   Alfred Dreyfus marries Lucie Hadamard (1870–1945).
            He is admitted to the Ecole supérieure de guerre.
1892   Dreyfus graduates from the Ecole supérieure de guerre,
            ninth of out a class of eighty-one.

1893

JAN. I   Dreyfus takes up his duties as an officer trainee at the
          General Staff of the French army.

1894

JULY 20   Major Ferdinand Walsin-Esterhazy offers his services
          to the German military attaché, Maximilian von
          Schwartzkoppen.

SEPT. 25 The document known as the bordereau arrives at the
          Ministry of War's Statistics Section (the General Staff's
          intelligence and counterintelligence bureau) through
          the "normal channel"—Madame Bastian, a cleaning
          woman employed by the German Embassy who is in
          the pay of the Statistics Section. She had removed it
          from Schwartzkoppen's wastebasket. The bordereau
          purports to document the delivery to Schwartzkoppen
          of French military secrets.

OCT. 6   After a rapid investigation, including a comparison
          by Major du Paty de Clam of Dreyfus's handwriting
          and the handwriting on the bordereau, the officers
          searching for the traitor who is the author of the
          document conclude that it is Dreyfus.

OCT. 15   Dreyfus is arrested on the charge of high treason and
          held incommunicado in the military prison on rue du
          Cherche-midi. Du Paty is put in charge of the pre-
          liminary secret investigation. Toward the end of the
          month, he reports to his superiors that the only evi-
          dence incriminating Dreyfus (the bordereau) is weak.

OCT. 31   The quasi-official news agency Havas discloses the
          arrest of a French officer on charges of spying. A daily
          newspaper, *Le Soir,* identifies Dreyfus as the officer
          who has been accused.

NOV. 1   A prominent article about Dreyfus appears in *La Libre Parole,* a rightist and anti-Semitic newspaper. A vehement campaign against Dreyfus begins in that newspaper and other similar publications, including *L'Intransigeant, Le Petit Journal,* and *L'Eclair,* which manifestly are receiving information leaked by Statistics Section officers in order to force the government to prosecute the Jewish "traitor."

NOV. 7   Dreyfus is made the subject of an official investigation. Three out of five handwriting experts consulted declare that the handwriting on the bordereau is his.

DEC. 19   The court-martial trial begins. Dreyfus's counsel is Edgar Demange. Over Demange's objections, *huis clos* (a closed trial) is imposed by the judges.

DEC. 22   On the last day of hearings, advised that the case is going badly for the prosecution, General Mercier, the minister of war, instructs du Paty to deliver secretly to the president of the tribunal a file of documents known as the dossier secret, with an order to show the documents to the other members of the tribunal. Included in the dossier are a copy of a letter from the Italian military attaché to Schwartzkoppen that refers to "that swine D." and a memorandum by du Paty that gives the contents of the dossier an incriminating slant. Neither Dreyfus nor Demange is informed of the existence or the delivery of the dossier. Apparently neither the military judges nor Major Picquart, who reports each day on the trial to the minister of war and General de Boisdeffre, the chief of staff, understands that the delivery of the dossier is a criminal violation of Dreyfus's rights.

The military judges unanimously find Dreyfus guilty and sentence him to military degradation, deportation, and imprisonment for life in a fortified place.

DEC. 31   Dreyfus's appeal from the court-martial judgment is rejected.

1895

JAN. 5   Dreyfus's degradation ceremony is held in the great courtyard of the Ecole militaire.

JAN. 15   Casimir Perier, the president of the French republic, resigns and is succeeded on January 17 by Félix Faure.

JAN. 17   Before surrendering his office, Mercier burns the du Paty memorandum included in the dossier secret in the presence of Lieutenant Colonel Sandherr, the chief of the Statistics Section, returns the rest of the dossier to him with instructions to place the documents in the files from which they had been taken, and requires his subordinates—Sandherr, General de Boisdeffre, General Gonse, du Paty, and Major Henry—to give him their word never to disclose what happened before and during the Dreyfus court-martial. He also orders the destruction of all other copies of the du Paty memorandum. Disobeying Mercier's order, Sandherr adds his personal copy of du Paty's memorandum to the dossier documents and places them all in a sealed envelope that he keeps in his office.

FEB. 21   Dreyfus boards the prison vessel that will transport him to Devil's Island.

At roughly the same time, President Faure explains to his friend and physician Dr. Joseph Gibert that Dreyfus was convicted on the basis of secret evidence delivered to the military judges, rather than because of the bordereau or anything that transpired at the trial. Gibert repeats this conversation to Mathieu Dreyfus, who is seeking a means of reversing the court-martial judgment and exonerating Alfred.

MARCH–
APRIL   Demange obtains from the minister of justice, Ludovic Trarieux, confirmation of the rumor that the military judges had seen a letter that referred to "that swine D."

JUNE   Mathieu Dreyfus engages Bernard Lazare, a rising young literary critic, to help him stimulate support for Alfred among writers and other intellectuals, and to prepare a memorandum demonstrating that Alfred was convicted as the result of a judicial error.

JULY 1   Lieutenant Colonel Georges Picquart replaces Sandherr as chief of the Statistics Section.

1896
FEB. 20   Esterhazy visits Schwartzkoppen at the German Embassy. The attaché expresses his dissatisfaction with Esterhazy's services and threatens to terminate their relationship.

EARLY
MARCH   An express letter (le petit bleu) addressed to Esterhazy is retrieved from Schwartzkoppen's wastebasket and delivered to the Statistics Section through the "normal channel." Recognizing its importance, Picquart places Esterhazy under police surveillance and begins to investigate his recent activities.

SUMMER   Having obtained samples of Esterhazy's handwriting Picquart compares it with the handwriting on the bordereau and realizes that they are identical. He also studies the documents in the dossier secret and determines that the dossier contains nothing of probative value. He is thus forced to conclude that Dreyfus is innocent, and the traitor is Esterhazy.

SEPT. 1 Picquart writes his first official report to his superiors setting forth his findings and subsequently attempts unsuccessfully to convince them of Dreyfus's innocence and Esterhazy's guilt. He urges Generals Gonse and de Boisdeffre to take prompt measures to correct the wrong done to Dreyfus for the sake of the army's reputation. The generals' attitude hardens: they wish to avoid at all costs judicial review of the 1894 court-martial.

SEPT. 3 A British newspaper falsely announces that Dreyfus has escaped from Devil's Island, a story planted by a journalist hired by Mathieu Dreyfus to keep the case before the public. The result is the imposition of a particularly cruel regime on Dreyfus, ostensibly to prevent an escape. For six weeks every night he is shackled to his bed.

SEPT. 9
AND 14 *L'Eclair,* a right-wing anti-Semitic newspaper, runs two articles concerning the delivery of the dossier secret to the military judges, its contents, and the approximate text of the bordereau. The paper's purpose is to dispel doubts about Dreyfus's guilt and squelch any tendency to feel sympathy for the traitor. The Sept. 15 article claims that the letter referring to "that swine D." is a clear reference to Dreyfus.

SEPT. 18 Dreyfus's wife, Lucie, petitions the Chamber of Deputies asking for judicial review of the court-martial's sentence on the basis of the *Eclair* revelations.

OCT. 27 General Billot, the minister of war, orders Picquart to go on an inspection tour of eastern France and Tunisia.

However, he does not specify a departure date.

NOV. 2 Major Henry of the Statistics Section, Picquart's second in command, gives General Gonse a letter purporting to be from the Italian military attaché to Schwartzkoppen that he has forged so as to irrefutably incriminate Dreyfus. The letter becomes known as the faux Henry. Although Picquart is still the titular head of the Statistics Section, neither Henry nor Gonse shows him the document, nor does the chief of staff, General de Boisdeffre.

NOV. 6 Bernard Lazare's pamphlet, *Une Erreur judiciaire: La Vérité sur l'Affaire Dreyfus* (A Judicial Error: The Truth About the Dreyfus Affair), is published and distributed widely to the French elites.

NOV. 10 *Le Matin,* a daily newspaper, publishes a facsimile of the bordereau. It reveals the illegal submission in 1894 of the dossier secret to the military judges and refers to the "that swine D." letter.

NOV. 16 Picquart leaves Paris.

DEC. 14 Henry forges the "Speranza" letter, mails it to Picquart, and intercepts it before it reaches the addressee. This is the first of the ambiguously worded forgeries that he sends to Picquart, intercepts, and shows to Gonse and Boisdeffre. They are used to discredit Picquart with the generals and to build a criminal case against him based on Henry's accusation that Picquart is in cahoots with the Dreyfus family and is leaking secret information.

1897

APRIL Picquart writes a codicil to his "testament," an exposé of what he has come to understand about the affair. He puts it and Gonse's letters to him in a sealed envelope that only the president of the republic is authorized to open.

JUNE   Picquart comes to Paris on leave and, concerned about Henry's plot against him, confides to his lawyer and friend Louis Leblois what he knows about Dreyfus's innocence and Esterhazy's guilt, but he does not tell him about the petit bleu. He gives Leblois the envelope intended for the president of the republic, authorizing him to reveal the information to a government official of his choice if necessary.

JULY 13   Leblois tells Auguste Scheurer-Kestner, the vice president of the Senate, everything he has learned from Picquart but puts onerous restrictions on Scheurer's use of the information. The next day Scheurer announces to colleagues in the Senate his intention to lead a campaign for Dreyfus's rehabilitation.

AUG.–
SEPT.   It becomes generally known among politicians and journalists that Scheurer believes that Dreyfus is innocent and is in possession of a file proving his case.

OCT. 17   A letter signed "Espérance" is sent to Esterhazy warning him of the accusations about to be leveled against him. The most likely author is Henry, dictating to his wife. This is the beginning of the Statistics Section's collaboration with the traitor and efforts to shield him, which will include secret contacts among Esterhazy, Henry, and du Paty.

END OF
OCT. –
EARLY
NOV.   Through contacts with Leblois and Scheurer, Emile Zola becomes convinced of Dreyfus's innocence and

throws himself into the struggle for his rehabilitation. J. de Castro, a securities dealer, sees a facsimile of the bordereau and recognizes the handwriting as that of Esterhazy, with whom he has had business dealings. He informs Mathieu Dreyfus.

NOV. 15   Mathieu Dreyfus denounces Esterhazy in a letter to General Billot, the minister of war. The text of the letter is made available to the press.

NOV. 17   General Billot orders a preliminary investigation of Esterhazy to be conducted by General Georges de Pellieux, who concludes that, while there is nothing to be held against Esterhazy, Picquart seems guilty. Pellieux bases his views on the "intercepted" forged telegrams and his perception that the petit bleu is not authentic.

NOV. 25   Aghast at the campaign of defamation against Scheurer in the nationalist and anti-Semitic press, Zola publishes a vigorous defense in *Le Figaro,* "M. Scheurer-Kestner." Five powerful essays demanding justice for Dreyfus will follow in the next two months.

DEC. 4   Notwithstanding General de Pellieux's finding, the minister of war orders a formal investigation of Esterhazy to be conducted by Major Ravary. That same day the minister gives a speech at the Chamber of Deputies declaring that Dreyfus had been justly convicted.

DEC. 7   Scheurer questions the government on the floor of the Senate about the Dreyfus Case, but his effort falls flat, having been upstaged by Billot.

DEC. 31   Ravary concludes that the proceeding against Esterhazy should be dismissed.

1898

JAN. 1   Esterhazy is ordered to stand trial by a court-martial,
          a measure he had requested with the encouragement
          of his handlers on the General Staff.

JAN. 4   Picquart files a criminal complaint against the un-
          known author or authors of the forged telegrams he
          has received.

JAN. 10–11 Esterhazy's court-martial is held, and he is acquitted
          by a unanimous verdict.

JAN. 13   Zola's "J'accuse" is published in the newspaper
          L'Aurore, of which Georges Clemenceau is the political
          editor. Picquart is sentenced to sixty days' imprison-
          ment, to be followed, as Pellieux had recommended,
          by a formal commission of inquiry.

FEB. 7   Zola's trial for libel against the court-martial officers
          begins. The defense manages to turn the General Staff
          and General Mercier into the real defendants.

FEB. 23   Zola is convicted and given the maximum sentence:
          one year in prison and a fine of 3,000 francs.

FEB. 24   In a hard-line speech before the Chamber of Deputies,
          Prime Minister Jules Méline declares the Dreyfus and
          Zola cases closed.

FEB. 26   Picquart is cashiered from the army by a 4 to 1 vote of
          the military commission.

APRIL 2   Zola's conviction is reversed on technical grounds.

MAY 23   Zola's second libel trial begins.

JUNE 28   A new cabinet is formed by Pierre Brisson with
          Godefroy Cavaignac as minister of war. Cavaignac is
          convinced of Dreyfus's guilt. He is hostile to Zola and
          Picquart, and intends to crush Dreyfusards by reveal-
          ing the secret documents that prove Dreyfus's guilt.

JULY 7   Cavaignac addresses the Chamber of Deputies, reading documents from the dossier secret, including the petit bleu, and threatens measures of repression against Dreyfusards. The speech is received enthusiastically, and posters reproducing its text are displayed across France by order of the Chamber.

JULY 8   Jean Jaurès publishes an open letter to Cavaignac in *La Petite République* announcing that he will refute every element of proof the minister of war has advanced. He makes good on his promise in a series of articles that appear through September 20. They are republished soon afterward in book form as *Les Preuves* (The Proofs).

JULY 9   Picquart writes to the prime minister offering to prove that two of the documents that Cavaignac read in the Chamber of Deputies do not concern Dreyfus and the third, the faux Henry, is a forgery. The letter is reproduced in the Parisian newspaper *Le Temps*.

JULY 12   Cavaignac files a criminal complaint against Picquart and Leblois, alleging that Picquart has given access to military secrets to the latter.

JULY 13   Picquart is arrested and imprisoned in the Santé prison in Paris.

JULY 18   Zola's second libel trial ends with his being again convicted and sentenced to one year of prison and a fine. He flees to London.

AUG. 13   One of Cavaignac's assistants, Captain Louis Cuignet, examines the faux Henry closely and determines that it is a forgery.

AUG. 30   Henry confesses to Cavaignac that he forged the faux Henry. Boisdeffre resigns from the army.

AUG. 31   Confined in the Mont-Valérien fortress, Henry commits suicide.

SEPT. 3	Cavaignac resigns as minister of war. Lucie Dreyfus petitions the government for judicial review of the 1894 court-martial judgment.
SEPT. 4	Having been cashiered from the army, Esterhazy flees to Belgium and from there to England.
SEPT. 21	Picquart is transferred from the civilian Santé prison to the military prison on rue du Cherche-midi to await court-martial on the charge of having forged the petit bleu.
SEPT. 26	After the successive resignations of three ministers of war unwilling to approve a petition by the government for review of the 1894 judgment, a new minister of war gives his approval, and the minister of justice finally transmits Lucie Dreyfus's petition to the Court of Cassation.
OCT. 29	The Court of Cassation orders a full investigation of the 1894 judgment.
NOV. 16	Dreyfus is notified by telegram that the petition has been accepted by the Court of Cassation. He is invited to prepare his defense.
1899	
JUNE 3	The united chamber of the Court of Cassation reverses the 1894 judgment and remands Dreyfus to a court-martial in Rennes.
JUNE 5	Zola returns to France.
JUNE 9	Dreyfus begins the voyage from Devil's Island to France aboard the cruiser *Sfax*. Picquart is allowed to leave the Santé prison, where he had been transferred in March from the Cherche-midi prison.
JUNE 13	Charges against Picquart and Leblois are dismissed.
JULY 1	Dreyfus lands in France and is transferred to the military prison in Rennes.

AUG. 8	The Rennes court-martial begins.
AUG. 14	Zola's and Dreyfus's lawyer Fernand Labori is fired upon and wounded; the assailant is never apprehended.
SEPT. 9	The military tribunal, by a 5 to 2 vote, finds Dreyfus guilty with extenuating circumstances and sentences him to ten years' imprisonment. The next day, the judges express the wish that he be spared a second military degradation.
SEPT. 19	Dreyfus receives a presidential pardon. He declares in a public statement his determination to continue the struggle to clear his name.

1900

| DEC. 14 | A law is passed granting amnesty for all crimes relating to the Dreyfus Affair. Dreyfus is excepted from the operation of the law so that he can pursue a review of the Rennes judgment. |

1902

| SEPT. 29 | Zola dies. |
| OCT. 5 | Zola is buried at the Montmartre cemetery. Anatole France pronounces the principal elegy. Dreyfus is present in spite of threats of violence against him. |

1904

| MARCH 5 | The Court of Cassation accepts the government's petition for review of the Rennes judgment on the ground of the discovery of new facts, including additional forgeries in the dossier presented to the military judges. |

1906

| JUNE 11 | The Court of Cassation votes unanimously to reverse the Rennes judgment, and 31 to 18 to do so without remand. The Court's judgment is read the next day in open court. |

JUNE 13   Legislation is passed reintegrating Dreyfus into the
army as a major, and Picquart as a brigadier general.

JUNE 20   Dreyfus is made a chevalier of the Legion of Honor in
a ceremony held in a courtyard of the Ecole militaire.

1907

JUNE 26   Dreyfus retires from the army.

1908

JUNE 4   Zola's remains are transferred to the Panthéon. Dreyfus, who attends the ceremony with his wife and children, is fired upon by an extremist right-wing journalist and wounded. The assailant is acquitted on the
ground that the attack was an act of passion and
therefore not premeditated.

1935

JULY 12   Dreyfus dies at his home in Paris.

notes

All translations from the French are mine unless otherwise identified.

CHAPTER ONE: "IF THEY HAVEN'T
BEEN ORDERED TO CONVICT HIM,
HE WILL BE ACQUITTED THIS
EVENING"

Title: Dreyfus's counsel, Edgar Demange, speaking to Mathieu Dreyfus immediately before the last session of the 1894 court-martial, quoted in Mathieu Dreyfus, *L'Affaire telle que je l'ai vécue* (Paris: Bernard Grasset, 1978), 43.

1. Maximilian von Schwartzkoppen, *Les Carnets de Schwartzkoppen (La Vérité sur Dreyfus),* ed. Bernhard Schwertfeger, trans. A. Koyré (Paris: Editions Rieder, 1930), 19.

2. Schwartzkoppen claimed that in fact he had never received the bordereau and advanced the theory that it had been stolen from his mailbox at the embassy by one of the agents of the Statistics Section and then torn into pieces to make it seem as though it had been retrieved from his wastebasket (*Carnets de Schwartzkoppen,* 24).

3. Maurice Paléologue, *Journal de l'Affaire Dreyfus, 1894–1899* (Paris: Librairie Plon, 1955), 7.

4. Ibid., 28.

5. Dreyfus memoir, quoted in Vincent Duclert, *Alfred Dreyfus: L'Honneur d'un patriote* (Paris: Fayard, 2006), 125.

6. Duclert, *Dreyfus*, 321. I am indebted to M. Duclert for the discussion of the run-up to the decision to proceed with the court-martial.

7. See Marcel Thomas, *L'Affaire sans Dreyfus* (Paris: Fayard, 1961), 137–39.

8. Schwartzkoppen, *Carnets de Schwartzkoppen*, 43–44.

9. Alfred Dreyfus, *Cinq années de ma vie* (1901; Paris: Maspero, 1982), 66.

10. Paléologue, *Journal de l'Affaire*, 105n1.

11. Ibid., 40.

12. Léon Blum, *Souvenirs sur l'Affaire* (Paris: Gallimard, 1981), 34.

13. Physicians for Human Rights, "Broken Laws, Broken Lives: Medical Evidence of Torture by the U.S.," http://brokenlives.info/?page_id=69 (accessed July 5, 2008); "Senate Armed Services Committee Inquiry into the Treatment of Detainees in U.S. Custody," http://www.armed-services.senate.gov/Publications/EXEC%20SUMMARY-CONCLUSIONS_For%20Release_12%20December%202008.pdf (accessed Dec. 20, 2008); U.S. Department of Defense news release, Dec. 16, 2008, http://www.defenselink.mil/releases/release.aspx?releaseid=12394 (accessed Dec. 30, 2008).

14. Mark Mazzetti, "CIA Destroyed Two Tapes Showing Interrogations," *New York Times,* Dec. 7, 2007; Michelle Shephard, "Ottawa Reverses Torture Stance," *Toronto Star,* Jan. 20, 2008, http://www.thestar.com/News/Canada/article/295706 (accessed Jan. 25, 2008); House of Commons Foreign Affairs Committee, *Human Rights Annual Report, 2007,* http://www.publications.parliament.uk/pa/cm200708/cmselect/cmfaff/533/533.pdf (accessed Aug. 1, 2008).

15. "Camp Delta Standard Operating Procedures (SOP)," https://secure.wikileaks.org/leak/gitmo-sop-2004.pdf (accessed Dec. 19, 2008); *Consigne pour le service de la déportation à l'Ile du Diable,* included in facsimile at the end of Dreyfus, *Cinq années de ma vie.*

16. Brookings Institution, "The Current Detainee Population of Guantánamo: An Empirical Study," http://www.brookings.edu/reports/2008/1216_detainees_wittes.aspx (accessed Dec. 30, 2008); order of Deputy Secretary of Defense Paul Wolfowitz, signed July 4, 2004, http://www.globalsecurity.org/security/library/policy/dod/d20040707review.pdf (accessed Dec. 30, 2008).

17. Firouz Sedarat, "Al Jazeera Cameraman Released from Guantanamo," *International Herald Tribune,* May 2, 2008, http://www.iht.com/articles/reuters/2008/05/02/africa/OUKWD-UK-USA-GUANTANAMO-JAZEERA.php (accessed Sept. 25, 2008).

18. *Mohammed El Gharani v. George W. Bush,* Memorandum Order, U.S. District Court for the District of Columbia, Jan. 14, 2009.

19. William Glaberson, "Panel Convicts bin Laden's Driver in Split Verdict," *New York Times,* Aug. 7, 2008, http://www.nytimes.com/2008/08/07/washington/07gitmo.html?_r=1&scp=6&sq=Salim%20Ahmed%20Hamdan&st=cse (accessed Dec. 22, 2008); Reuters, "Yemen Releases Former bin Laden Driver from Jail," *New York Times,* Jan. 12, 2009, http://www.nytimes.com/2009/01/12/world/middleeast/12yemen.html?scp=7&sq=Salim%20Ahmed%20Hamdan&st=cse (Jan. 15, 2009).

20. William Glaberson, "Case Against 9/11 Detainee Is Dismissed, *New York Times,* May 14, 2008, http://www.nytimes.com/2008/05/14/washington/14gitmo.html (accessed May 25, 2008); Bob Woodward, "Detainee Tortured, Says U.S. Official," *Washington Post,* Jan. 13, 2009, http://www.washingtonpost.com/wp-dyn/content/article/2009/01/13/AR2009011303372.html (accessed Jan. 15 2009).

21. "Former Guard on Guantanamo 'Torture,'" *BBC News,* Jan. 9, 2009, http://news.bbc.co.uk/2/hi/americas/7821569.stm (accessed Jan. 11, 2009).

22. William Glaberson, "5 Charged in 9/11 Attacks Seek to Plead Guilty," *New York Times,* Dec. 9, 2008, http://www.nytimes.com/2008/12/09/us/09gitmo.html?pagewanted=2&emc=eta1 (accessed Dec. 12, 2008).

23. Quinnipiac University, "November 12, 2008—Voters Say 'Yes We Can' with High Hopes for Obama, Quinnipiac University National Poll Finds; But Most Voters Say He Won't Cut Taxes," Nov. 12, 2008, http://www.quinnipiac.edu/x1295.xml?ReleaseID=1228 (accessed Nov. 20, 2008).

CHAPTER TWO: "THE PAST IS NEVER DEAD"

Title: William Faulkner, *Requiem for a Nun.*

1. Charles de Gaulle, *La France et son armée* (Paris: Plon, 1971), 224. I am deeply indebted in the discussion of the Franco-Prussian War to Professor Geoffrey Wawro. See generally Wawro, *The Franco-Prussian War: The German Conquest of France in 1870–1871* (Cambridge: Cambridge University Press, 2003). Paine's pamphlet became an instant best seller in the American colonies and Europe.

2. Because the king had written to Bismarck from Bad Ems, where he had been taking the waters, Bismarck's version of the king's cable became known as the Bad Ems dispatch.

3. Marcel Thomas, *L'Affaire sans Dreyfus* (Paris: Fayard, 1961), 162.

4. De Gaulle, *La France et son armée,* 231.

5. See Alfred Dreyfus, *Cinq années de ma vie* (1901; Paris: Maspero, 1982), and Mathieu Dreyfus, *L'Affaire telle que je l'ai vécue* (Paris: Grasset, 1978).

6. Only estimates of the Jewish population are available because since 1872 the census has excluded questions concerning religion. In addition, some forty-five thousand Jews lived in Algeria, and Algerian Jews were granted French citizenship in 1870. There had been Jewish

students at the Ecole polytechnique since its first graduating class (1794). Dreyfus had had four Jewish classmates, two of whom were sons of rabbis (Félix Perez, "Sociologie des élèves juifs reçus à l'X, 1794–1927," http://judaisme.sdv.fr/perso/polytech/polytech.htm [accessed Aug. 26, 2008]).

7. Joseph Reinach, *Histoire de l'Affaire Dreyfus*, 6 vols. (Paris: Revue blanche, 1901–8).

8. A gripping description of what it might have been like to be a Jewish medical officer in the Austro-Hungarian army can be found in Joseph Roth, *The Radetzky March*, trans. Geoffrey Dunlop (London: Penguin, 1974).

9. For the discussion in the present paragraph I am deeply indebted to Professor Michael R. Marrus. See Marrus, *The Politics of Assimilation: The French Jewish Community at the Time of the Dreyfus Affair* (Oxford: Clarendon, 1971).

10. Léon Blum, *Souvenirs sur l'Affaire* (Paris: Gallimard, 1981), 42–43, ellipsis in original.

11. Marrus, *Politics of Assimilation*, 208–9.

12. Charles Péguy, *Notre jeunesse* (Paris: Gallimard, 1957), 87.

13. Léon Daudet, *Panorama de la IIIe République, 1870–1936* (Paris: Gallimard, 1936), 186.

CHAPTER THREE: "WHAT DO YOU CARE IF THAT JEW STAYS ON DEVIL'S ISLAND?"

Title: General Arthur Gonse to Lieutenant Colonel Georges Picquart, quoted in Marcel Thomas, *L'Affaire sans Dreyfus* (Paris: Fayard, 1961), 280.

1. Mathieu Dreyfus, *L'Affaire telle que je l'ai vécue* (Paris: Fayard, 1971), 47.

2. Léon Blum, *Souvenirs sur l'Affaire* (Paris: Gallimard, 1981), 40.

3. M. Dreyfus, *L'Affaire telle que je l'ai vécue,* 83.

4. Bernard Lazare, *Une Erreur judiciaire: La Vérité sur l'Affaire Dreyfus* (Paris: P.-V. Stock, 1897). Michael R. Marrus, one of the best historians of the period, notes that "had it not been for the publication of Lazare's . . . brochure . . . the Affair itself might have been forgotten" (Marrus, *The Politics of Assimilation: The French Jewish Community at the Time of the Dreyfus Affair* [Oxford: Clarendon, 1971], 206).

5. See Francis de Pressensé, *Un Héro—Le Colonel Picquart* (Paris: P.-V. Stock, 1899). Pressensé was a French diplomat, journalist, and socialist politician, as well as the author of several works on history and politics.

6. Maurice Paléologue, *Journal de l'Affaire Dreyfus, 1894–1899* (Paris: Librairie Plon, 1955), 53–54.

7. At the degradation ceremony Picquart apparently gave the following answer to a fellow officer who asked him why Dreyfus paid such close attention when the gold braid was torn off his uniform: "He was thinking about their weight: so many grams at such and such price, comes to so much" (Thomas, *L'Affaire sans Dreyfus,* 235n32).

8. Quoted ibid., 192.

9. Ibid.

10. Maximilian von Schwartzkoppen, *Les Carnets de Schwartzkoppen (La Vérité sur Dreyfus),* ed. Bernhard Schwertfeger, trans. A. Koyré (Paris: Editions Rieder, 1930), 139–40.

11. Quoted in Thomas, *L'Affaire sans Dreyfus,* 244, 248.

12. Quoted ibid., 280.

13. Paléologue, *Journal de l'Affaire,* 55.

14. Ibid., 138–39.

15. Quoted in Thomas, *L'Affaire sans Dreyfus,* 295 (ellipses in original).

16. Quoted ibid., 299.

17. Quoted ibid., 325.

18. Ferdinand Walsin-Esterhazy, *Les Dessous de l'Affaire Dreyfus* (Paris: Fayard Frères, 1898), 144.

19. Paléologue, *Journal de l'Affaire,* 219–20.

Title : "Monsieur Scheurer-Kestner," *Le Figaro,* November 25, 1897, collected in Emile Zola, *La Vérité en marche: L'Affaire Dreyfus,* ed. Colette Becker (Paris: Flammarion, 1969), 123.

1. Zola, *La Vérité en marche,* 55.

2. Ibid., 73, 81, 89, 99.

3. Quoted in Marcel Thomas, *L'Affaire sans Dreyfus* (Paris: Fayard, 1961), 437 (ellipses in the original). "Uhlan" was the name given to Prussian cavalry.

4. Quoted ibid., 444.

5. Zola, *La Vérité en marche,* 111.

6. Ibid., 124.

7. Article 35, Loi du 29 juillet 1881 sur la liberté de la presse, "Grandes lois de la République," http://mjp.univ-perp.fr/france/1881presse.htm (accessed Jan. 20, 2009).

8. Léon Blum, *Souvenirs sur l'Affaire* (Paris: Gallimard, 1981), 126.

9. Quoted in Thomas, *L'Affaire sans Dreyfus,* 453–54.

10. The prices realized in the sale auction in March 1903 of nine early Cézannes that had belonged to Zola ranged from 600 to 4,200 francs; see Frederick Brown, *Zola: A Life* (New York: Farrar, Straus and Giroux, 1995), 800n2.

11. Maurice Paléologue, *Journal de l'Affaire Dreyfus, 1894–1899* (Paris: Librairie Plon, 1955), 110–12.

12. Mathieu Dreyfus, *L'Affaire telle que je l'ai vécue* (Paris: Fayard, 1971), 117–18.

13. Quoted in Thomas, *L'Affaire sans Dreyfus*, 461.

14. Quoted ibid., 161.

15. Paléologue, *Journal de l'Affaire*, 125, 134.

16. Quoted in Blum, *Souvenirs sur l'Affaire*, 133; Jean Jaurès, *Les Preuves: L'Affaire Dreyfus* (Paris: Editions La Découverte, 1998).

17. Quoted in Thomas, *L'Affaire sans Dreyfus*, 466; Jean Denis Bredin, *L'Affaire* (Paris: Julliard, 1983), 310.

18. Quoted in Thomas, *L'Affaire sans Dreyfus*, 467.

19. Bredin, *L'Affaire*, 324–25.

20. Paléologue, *Journal de l'Affaire*, 172.

21. See Loi du 29 juillet 1881 sur la liberté de la presse, Article 38; question for the court-martial quoted in Bredin, *L'Affaire*, 355.

22. Alfred Dreyfus, *Cinq années de ma vie* (1901; Paris: Maspero, 1982), 202–3.

23. Ibid., 205.

24. Ibid., 212.

25. Ibid., 213.

26. Paléologue, *Journal de l'Affaire*, 197.

27. Quoted in Michael Burns, *France and the Dreyfus Affair* (Boston: St. Martin's, 1999), 153–54.

28. Paléologue, *Journal de l'Affaire*, 262.

29. Alfred Dreyfus, *Carnets, 1899–1906* (Paris: Calmann-Lévy, 1998), 173; Paléologue, *Journal de l'Affaire*, 223.

30. Quoted in Burns, *France and the Dreyfus Affair*, 152.

31. Paléologue, *Journal de l'Affaire*, 193, 210–11, 263 (ellipses in original).

32. Ibid., 264.

33. Ibid., 222.

34. Quoted in M. Dreyfus, *L'Affaire telle que je l'ai vécue,* 243.

35. Charles Péguy, *Notre jeunesse* (Paris: Gallimard, 1957), 76.

36. Ibid., 76.

37. Ibid., 232–33.

38. Quoted in Bredin, *L'Affaire,* 399–400.

39. Zola, *La Vérité en marche,* 159.

40. Quoted in A. Dreyfus, *Carnets,* 261.

41. A. Dreyfus, *Carnets,* 273.

42. Franz Kafka, *Letters to Milena,* trans. Philip Boehm (New York: Schocken, 1990), 212–13.

CHAPTER FIVE: "DREYFUS WAS REHABILITATED, PICQUART BECAME MINISTER OF WAR, AND NOBODY SAID BOO"

Title: Marcel Proust, *Le Temps retrouvé,* vol. 7 of Proust, *A la recherche du temps perdu* (Paris: Robert Lafont, 1987), 649.

1. Léon Blum, *Souvenirs sur l'Affaire* (Paris: Gallimard, 1981), 78; Anatole France, *L'Ile des pingouins* (Paris: Calmann-Lévy, 1927); France, *L'Anneau d'améthyste* (Paris: Calmann-Lévy, 1899); France, *M. Bergeret à Paris* (Paris: Calmann-Lévy, 1901). Roger Martin du Gard (1881–1958), a great novelist and Nobel Prize winner best known for the nine-volume cycle *Les Thibault* (1921–40), made the affair one of the principal themes of *Jean Barois.* First published in 1913, *Jean Barois* was very successful, though today it seems heavily programmatic and wooden.

2. Marcel Proust, *Jean Santeuil* (Paris: Gallimard Quarto, 2001), 567–69.

3. Ibid., 603.

4. Marcel Proust, *La Fugitive,* vol. 6 of Proust, *A la recherche du temps perdu,* 471.

5. Marcel Proust, *Le Côté de Guermantes,* vol. 3 of Proust, *A la recherche du temps perdu,* 220, 226.

6. Ibid., 594.

index

Until his retirement in 2004, Louis Begley was a senior partner at Debevoise & Plimpton, where he practiced law for forty-five years. Begley's fiction, including *Wartime Lies, About Schmidt,* and *Matters of Honor,* has been translated into fifteen languages. He is a recipient of numerous literary awards including the PEN/Hemingway Award, the Irish Times/Aer Lingus International Fiction Award, the Prix Médicis étranger, and the American Academy of Arts and Letters Award in Literature.